TEAM DRILLS
— FOR —
HOCKEY

Dr. Randy Gregg

OVER
TIME
BOOKS

© 2006 by OverTime Books
First printed in 2006   10 9 8 7 6 5 4 3 2 1
Printed in Canada

The Publisher: OverTime Books is an imprint of Éditions de la Montagne Verte

Library and Archives Canada Cataloguing in Publication

Gregg, Randy, 1956–
    Team drills for hockey / Randy Gregg.

    ISBN-13: 978-0-9737681-7-6
    ISBN-10: 0-9737681-7-7

    1. Hockey—Coaching. I. Title.

GV848.3.G749 2006   796.962077   C2006-904207-1

Project Director: J. Alexander Poulton
Illustrator: Ross Palsson
Cover Image: Dave Vasicek, ColorSpace Photo-Graphics

PC:P5

Dedication

To my daughter Jessica,
whose smiling face during the heat of competition
reaffirms my belief that sport should first and
foremost be great fun for all involved

Contents

Skills-Based Learning

LIKE MOST TEAM SPORTS, HOCKEY IS AN INTEGRATED GAME. Players must learn the individual skills necessary to be a competent player. A young athlete must then learn how to use these skills in a team environment so that team performance is maximized. As a player progresses to a more competitive hockey environment, there is an increased emphasis on physical conditioning using on-ice and dryland training. However, in addition to skill mastery and the physical part of the game, it is mental strength that can often separate elite hockey players from true superstars.

Although the individual abilities of hockey players vary widely from youth to adolescence to adulthood, the skills they must possess to become better are similar. There are 10 skills that are of primary importance in the development of a hockey player. These include skating speed, agility, power, stickhandling, passing, shooting, checking, positional play, intuition and work ethic. It is important to emphasize the development of these skills at every practice.

In organized minor hockey, players are seldom coached by the same person for more than one season. Inevitably, each year players must adapt to yet another coaching style and temperament. This may not be such a bad thing because it gives the young players a wide range of experience so they can judge for themselves what type of coach or practice makes them perform at optimal levels. However, the main problem with exposing young players to a different coach every year is the variability in how each one teaches the 10 fundamental hockey skills.

An analogy with formal schooling is appropriate. Does a Grade Four math teacher develop and teach a system of learning to calculate fractions only to have the Grade Five teacher create a completely new system? Of course not. The school system was developed with an organized, consistent approach to learning so that students get the best chance to excel in all the subjects. Curricula are established and then closely followed by teachers from year to year so that every child has an equal opportunity to learn.

In hockey, well-meaning and enthusiastic volunteers give their time freely "to help the kids." Without volunteer coaching ranks, it would not be possible for the vast majority of youngsters to play hockey. Thirty years ago, Father David Bauer believed that it would be best if hockey was integrated into the school system to ensure consistent instruction for all players. Over the years there have been a number of excellent programs for coaches to become even better teachers on the ice. I hope that this manual can provide some valuable tools that will make this directed focus on teaching at practice even more successful.

SKILLS-BASED LEARNING

How to Use this Book

IN VIRTUALLY EVERY ASPECT OF SOCIETY, PREPARATION and planning are two vital steps toward success in any endeavor. Teachers prepare lesson plans for their daily classes, doctors prepare for surgical procedures and truck drivers plan their routes before embarking on a trip. Similarly, it is imperative that coaches plan and prepare for each practice. Having an overall objective for each practice is essential. The objective for a particular practice may be skating, breakouts, power play or defensive zone play, but it is important that the objectives for individual practices also further the overall goal of building a team that works well together. It is important to select practice drills that best suit the needs of the team at that particular stage of the season. This book describes many team drills that can be used to develop a strong practice plan. Skating, puck control, advanced and goalie drills can be found in Books 1, 2 and 4.

Five Guidelines for Practice Planning

When developing a practice plan, follow these five main guidelines in order to maximize a team's practice potential:

1.	Be prepared—make a practice plan.
2.	Use progressive skill learning through drill expansion.
3.	Work on each individual skill during each practice.
4.	Use technical and dynamic drills in appropriate situations.
5.	Make practices fun.

Be prepared—make a practice plan

Coaches expect every player to come to practice with skates, stick and other equipment in hand, ready to work hard for the entire one-hour practice. Similarly, players and parents should expect the coaching staff to be ready to run an effective, well-organized practice with drills that challenge and stimulate players in every position. As in many other teaching professions, a written plan is a valuable tool for two reasons:

1. Making a practice plan requires that a coach spend time the night before thinking about the strengths and weaknesses of his team and how it can improve. Then the coach can choose specific drills to focus on learning in those areas of weakness. A written practice plan is easy to follow and provides a focus for the practice, ensuring that ice time is used most efficiently.

2. Watching a coach who regularly checks his written plan gives parents in the stands confidence that the practice has been well thought through and will be worthwhile for their children. Demonstrating a high level of preparation is an important step to gaining their confidence towards the decisions made during each game of the season.

Use progressive skill learning through drill expansion

Shortly after retiring from the National Hockey League, I had the opportunity to coach my young sons in organized youth hockey. Although it was quite obvious that their skill level was low, I tried the same drills that I had used in NHL practices. Of course, I had to scale back both the complexity and intensity of the drills to fit the level of my little team. I was pleased to see that, not only did these young seven- and eight-year-olds pick up the idea behind the drills quickly, but practices were high paced, fun and a wealth of learning for the players. I realized then that the skills of hockey are no different whether at the atom or the professional level. It was simply a matter of establishing the level of complexity that could be handled by the players in question. The concept of drill expansion was born. It excited me to think that young hockey players could go through their entire minor hockey experience practicing a set of drills that were consistent yet constantly expanding in intensity and complexity. Novice players, Bantam players and Olympians can use a similar set of drills that provide a consistent approach to teaching the skills of the game. This idea is, of course, no different than what the school system did years ago when they developed standardized teaching curricula in the core school subjects so that all students benefit from formal education. That has always sounded like a worthy goal for hockey organizations. However, because the system relies on volunteer coaches who have diverse backgrounds and who often change from year to year, the idea of a common coaching strategy with regards to practice organization is still in its infancy.

The Canadian Hockey Association and USA Hockey have done a remarkable job in developing coaching seminars and-clinics to provide coaches with a stronger background in-hockey knowledge. This book is intended to be a useful, practical tool for coaches interested in offering the best practices available to their players. Sample practice plans and practice templates have been included in the book to make it easy for a coach at any hockey level to expand his skills in practice planning and organization. Refer to *Skating Drills for Hockey* (Book 1), *Puck Control Drills for Hockey* (Book 2) and *Advanced Drills & Goalie Drills for Hockey* (Book 4) for other drills to complete your practice.

Work on each individual skill during each practice

Having a major theme or objective in mind is a good idea when planning a hockey practice. If the team is struggling with passing or defensive positioning, then it would be productive to include specific drills that focus on those areas. It is also important to consider including at least one drill to work each of the specific individual hockey skills while progressing through practice. Following a good warmup, it is important to work on skating, stickhandling, passing, shooting and checking skills in every practice before requiring players to perform the more dynamic team-oriented drills. It has been said a solid house is built on a strong foundation and there is no doubt that the foundation of a good hockey player is the mastery of individual technical skills!

Use technical and dynamic drills effectively

Because teaching the various aspects of the game of hockey can be complicated in both its individual and team responsibilities, it is important that coaches help players develop new skills in a slow and progressive way. Attempting to teach a sophisticated defensive breakout system to a group of first-year players is a recipe for disaster. Fortunately, most hockey skills can be taught in two ways— technically and dynamically.

In this manual you will notice that the drills are divided into two basic groupings:

- **Technical drills** are designed to decrease the complexity of the rink environment so that players can focus totally on one specific skill. This is a time when coaches can easily approach individual players to work on teaching changes to their technique in a particular area. A good example of a technical drill would be the Stationary Pass Drill, where players stand in one location working with a partner on receiving and making good passes.

- **Dynamic drills** are designed to integrate the exciting aspects of hockey, including speed, finesse, positional play and checking. These drills are effective in developing the same individual technical skills but are set in an environment that more closely resembles a regular game setting. Because these drills are run at a faster pace, several external stimuli are present that challenge each player to be even more aware of the entire game setting. Do not try dynamic drills until all players have almost mastered the technical drills that teach similar hockey skills in isolation. For more experienced players, this kind of drill most closely simulates game situations where many things are happening on the ice at one time.

Drill Favorites Icon: Several drills in the book are identified with this icon. These are my favorite drills in each of the skill sections. They are drills that are applicable at any age level in hockey, and I strongly recommend them to any coach. Even the best hockey coach does not need thousands of drills in order to improve his team. He simply needs a core of ten or twenty drills that he feels comfortable with to properly develop his players' individual and team skills.

 Level of Difficulty Icon: All of the drills in this book have been assigned a level of difficulty, which provides a sense of how and when a particular drill should be included in planning a practice. A drill with Level 1 difficulty can be easily carried out by beginning players, while a drill with Level 4 difficulty is quite complex and should be reserved for more experienced, competitive players.

It is necessary to first evaluate the level of talent on the team. From that assessment, determine the level of difficulty that is most appropriate for the drills to include in a practice plan.

Make practices fun

There continues to be a small group of coaches, managers and parents who believe that players cannot develop the ultimate commitment to hockey if they have fun during practice. A smiling, joking player who enjoys the social aspect of hockey to the same degree as he enjoys the physical aspect has in the past been looked upon as being soft or lacking discipline. Luckily, this attitude is quickly going the way of the dinosaur!

For the vast majority of amateur hockey players, the number one reason why they play hockey is to have fun with their friends. Although many dream of a professional career, the reality for most is that success will likely be measured by simply continuing through the minor hockey ranks and enjoying the game so much that they continue to play into adulthood. Hockey is a fine game with its speed, finesse, tactics and emphasis on teamwork. Every child who is interested should have the opportunity to participate in the game at a level that is best suited for him skillwise, socially, and financially.

Coaches who berate players, punish them with excessive skating or who verbally criticize young referees in front of their teams have little grasp of the great influence they really have on their players. Hockey continues to struggle to keep its players from turning to sports that offer recreation at a lower cost. Many hockey experts believe that a major turnaround in attitude towards the teaching of hockey is needed in order to return hockey to its position of glory in the cultural makeup of our country.

So what can a coach do to ensure that each player on his team enjoys the sport of hockey to its utmost? From a psychological standpoint, there are many ways a coach can help build self-esteem, create a non-threatening dressing room environment and assist in developing long-term friendships among the team members. Unfortunately, this topic is outside the scope of this book. For further details and a more comprehensive reference on coaching philosophy, injury identification, proper nutrition and skill enhancement, please refer to *Hockey: The Technical, the Physical, and the Mental Game.**

Every morning on a game day, National Hockey League teams have a pre-game skate. It is usually just a quick workout so that players can stretch out and work on some flow drills before the evening game. During my time with the Edmonton Oilers, the real practice often began once the coaches left the ice. Players would surround the center ice circle and begin a rousing game of Pig in the Middle. We would play that game for what seemed like hours, working on our passing and receiving, but mostly just having a great time. The memories of players like Gretzky and Messier laughing and joking during the simple game that I now use with my young teams will stay with me forever. Many people wonder why some players become truly great superstars. Part of the puzzle is undoubtedly physical talent, but I am sure that a big part of hockey success also comes from this intense love of playing the game.

---

* *Hockey: The Technical, the Physical, and the Mental Game* by Dr. Randy Gregg.
©1999, FP Hendriks Publishing Ltd.

During practices coaches can do several things to ensure that players enjoy their hockey experience:

1. **Have a positive attitude.**
   Every hockey player makes mistakes. If we focus on what people can do rather than what they can't, then we develop willing and eager players.

2. **Maintain a high tempo at practice.**
   One easy way that players lose interest in the game is when they must endure a poorly organized and boring practice. Make it fast and make it fun!

3. **Lead by example; be energetic.**
   It's hard for a player to give all he has if his coach and role model is lethargic, bored and appears to be disinterested.

4. **Be fair.**
   The quickest way to lose your players' respect is to show favoritism to your own child or to the players on the team who are more skilled.

5. **Run practices efficiently.**
   The main reason coaches must extend practices for minor hockey players past one hour is because they are not well prepared. Short, high-tempo practices make for good skill challenges and happy players!

6. **Include at least one fun drill at the end of practice.**
   Would you rather have your players spend the three or four days before next practice remembering how sick they felt after a hard punishing skate, or would you rather they remember the excitement and fun of playing a challenging game that also helped to improve their hockey skills? The answer seems obvious to most. Please refer to Book 4, *Advanced Drills & Goalie Drills for Hockey*, for some effective ideas that can be used during each practice.

A Note about Male and Female Hockey

You will notice throughout this book that I use the words *he*, *him*, and *his* when describing hockey players and coaches. I do this only for ease of reading, not because of a bias towards male dominance in hockey. It is exciting to see the number of female hockey teams sprouting up in amateur hockey leagues across the country, as well as the development of many very capable and experienced female coaches. Hockey is the type of dynamic, fast-paced game that should be enjoyed by all youngsters, big or small, rich or poor, skilled or inexperienced, male or female. It is encouraging to see interest in female hockey increase, from novice levels all the way up to participation in the Olympic Games!

> *Even the best hockey coach does not need thousands of drills in order to improve his team. He simply needs a core of 10 or 20 drills that he feels comfortable with to properly develop his players' individual and team skills.*

Skill Development

BECAUSE IT IS A GAME OF HIGH SPEED, PHYSICAL CONTACT and fast-paced action, hockey demands many specialized skills from its participants. One of the main responsibilities of a coach is to help players develop these skills through good practice organization, assessment and positive feedback. Before plunging into teaching specific hockey skills, however, it is important to gain a perspective on skill development. There are two ways to do this:

1. Separate the game into its basic components.
2. Teach skills progressively.

School teachers know the most effective ways to teach children valuable educational information. The wide scope of information that children must learn in school includes reading and writing skills, mathematics, science and social studies. These academic subjects (or information groups) have been artificially separated to make it easier for a student to learn and understand information. Too much information overwhelms rather than informs. Can you imagine a teacher in the middle of a science lesson abruptly switching gears and giving out a math assignment? Only when a student becomes more experienced and mature is it appropriate to combine all the educational components, forming a mosaic of overall learning. Sounds a little bit like coaching hockey!

Before teaching skills in isolation, however, it is important to place the teaching of those skills into an overall perspective. Any experienced hockey person can teach the skills listed; however, it is often the way these skills are taught that makes the difference between success on the ice and a frustrated group of players who have the skills but have an incomplete understanding of how to apply them in a game situation. Players gain an understanding of the way the game works and can apply specific skills when coaches

1. teach the basic components of the game and
2. teach skills progressively.

Teach the Basic Components of the Game

It is important for coaches to divide the sometimes confusing game of hockey into its specific components, especially for young players. For example, most players would probably say that they prefer to scrimmage for the whole practice. They consider it to be the most fun. However, playing a game or scrimmaging involves the integration of many skills. For a developing player, a scrimmage is a difficult environment for learning and one in which poor habits are easily acquired. With so many actions and developing plays all over the ice during a scrimmage, it is more difficult to single out specifics for learning purposes. By separating the many skills required in a scrimmage into individual components that can more easily be practiced in isolation, coaches can foster good habits and slowly build on what players have learned so that the game becomes a more dynamic challenge for players.

Even experienced players benefit from practices where the focus is on isolated skills such as speed, agility or the power components of skating. As the players' skills become more developed, coaches can slowly integrate two skills into a particular practice drill, then three and so on. Soon players are able to practice more complex drills that closely simulate game situations. More important though, players develop improved hockey skills and are less likely to acquire bad habits or miss the essential elements that make up a well-rounded hockey player.

SKILL DEVELOPMENT

Teach Skills Progressively

Keep in mind the teaching strategies that are used each weekday in school classrooms everywhere. The curriculum outlines levels of learning, concepts and skills that are appropriate for the children of a certain age or grade in specific subjects, such as math, science, language arts or physical education. Teachers then write year plans, unit plans and daily lesson plans to teach students these skills and concepts. Once the desired level of learning is attained, teachers then reset their teaching goals to a higher level and begin to further stimulate the students into expanding their knowledge base. Called progressive learning, this highly developed process begins in kindergarten and continues through elementary, junior high, high school and on into postsecondary learning.

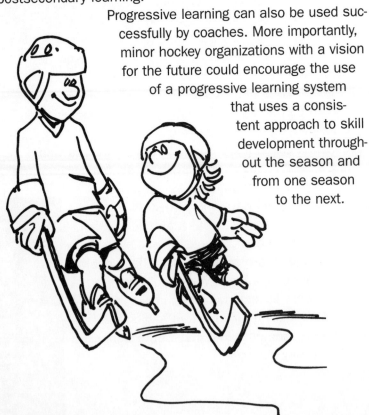

Progressive learning can also be used successfully by coaches. More importantly, minor hockey organizations with a vision for the future could encourage the use of a progressive learning system that uses a consistent approach to skill development throughout the season and from one season to the next.

Valuable learning opportunities and highly developed skills are enhanced in minor hockey when established and progressive drill and practice patterns are used consistently by all coaches. Having each coach trying to teach hockey drills in a unique way does not accomplish nearly as much. A consistent approach eliminates the need for players to learn and to adapt to an all-new set of drills, terms and practice dynamics at the beginning of each season.

Of course, players benefit from exposure to a variety of coaching styles. Every player is likely to be taught by quiet, reserved coaches, more aggressive, motivating individuals, as well as by coaches who love to yell and scream. As a result of this varied exposure, athletes form attitudes about how different coaching styles affect them. They will develop their own sense of coaching tactics and attitudes that they will eventually use when they become team leaders. While exposure to various coaching techniques and philosophies can be worthwhile, unfortunately it often brings with it a yearly change in fundamental skill teaching and practice organization. It is a huge and daunting task to ask hockey coaches to agree to replace their personal drills and practice organization with a consistent across-the-board organizational approach. However, for the ultimate benefit of young players in that organization, it is well worth the effort!

Consider the difference in outcome for an eight-year-old novice entering a minor hockey program committed to a consistent skill and practice development program. After eight years, this young athlete will have had the benefit of an amazing learning experience, all because of a commitment to excellence at the organizational level!

Team Drills

IN ORDER TO BUILD A SOLID AND COMFORTABLE HOUSE, carpenters must first build a strong foundation on which to put the wall, window, doors and roof. Similarly, the development of a well-rounded player depends on building a strong foundation with individual skills such as skating, stickhandling, passing and shooting. Once a player learns these skills, a good coach has the opportunity to show that player how to use those skills to help make the team more successful.

It has been said that hockey is a game of five one-on-ones all over the ice, and the team that wins the most one-on-one battles will ultimately be victorious. I believe that concept to be true, because good physical skills are needed to compete at a high level in hockey. In addition, a group of players who can work together as a unit under the guidance of their

coach will be more effective. A strong team concept tends to lessen individual skill weaknesses and augment the strength that each player brings to the game. The development of a consistent team concept from a group of skilled players is the ultimate challenge for all coaches, and in almost all cases, the most important challenge.

The skills to be developed in a team approach to hockey are:

- checking,
- defensive zone skills and
- offensive zone skills.

This book also contains sections on attitude for players as well as tips for coaching.

TEAM DRILLS

Checking

Checking

Definition—*the ability to use a stick or the body to separate the opposing player from the puck*

MANY HOCKEY FANS ASSOCIATE CHECKING WITH THOSE blistering mid-ice hip checks that are spectacular to watch. They are indeed exciting; however, at the youth hockey level they are frequently done improperly. It is important that coaches feel comfortable teaching young players the many different strategies for taking the puck off an opposing player.

Checking is a skill that is used hundreds of times during a game, even in games with young players where the rules disallow body contact. It includes poke checks, sweep checks, stick checks, angling, boards pinning, as well as the more aggressive shoulder and hip checks. Although some minor hockey organizations do not allow body checking before age 12, it is important that players of all ages begin to master the various checking techniques that are used during a game. Slow controlled checking drills can progress to more dynamic drills that are both physically challenging and instructive for all players. It is crucial that this progression is done at a rate that suits all the players on the team so that no player feels intimidated, alienated from, or uncomfortable with the physical contact component of hockey.

On the following pages are drills that focus on checking skills. Taught properly, the many components of checking in hockey can make the game even more enjoyable for young athletes, instead of being the main reason some quit playing so early in life.

Angling Check

Poke Check

Hip Check

Sweep Check

Shoulder Check

One-on-One Defensive Positioning

CHECKING

One-on-One Stationary Keepaway

Objective
To develop proper positioning and stability while protecting the puck

Description
- Pair up players of equal ability and size in the neutral zone.
- Provide each pair with one puck that is left stationary on the ice.
- One player protects the puck from the other but does not move the puck.
- The puck defender tries to keep his opponent off his strong shoulder, that is, the shoulder that controls the lower hand on the stick. This technique allows for better leverage of the stick, if necessary, during the one-on-one drill.
- Both players face the puck, moving laterally as needed.
- The attacker tries to fake and make quick lateral movements to get by the defender and reach the puck.
- Begin and end the drill with a whistle to ensure high intensity.

Key Teaching Points
- Encourage players to keep the opposing players controlled off their strong shoulders (the shoulder that controls the lower hand on the stick).
- Promote a tripod stance with knees bent to maximize strength.
- Control the drill with a whistle to ensure high intensity at all times.

EXPANSION
The defensive player plays without a stick to increase the challenge.

**ONE-ON-ONE
STATIONARY KEEPAWAY**

Angle Boards Checking

Objective
To develop the ability to properly angle an opposing player into the boards

Description
- Divide the players into two lines in one corner of the ice, one near the boards and the other farther out.
- On a whistle, the skater nearest the boards moves slowly along the boards.
- The inside player slowly narrows the gap and takes the skater out of the play. To effectively angle a player off, the inside arm is placed in front of the player, the inside leg is placed behind the player, and the pressure to pin strongly comes from bent legs.
- Players change positions after every angling attempt.

Key Teaching Points
- Perform the drill at half speed only.
- Ensure there is no solid contact; players work only on technique.
- Ensure good control of the drill by the coaches.

EXPANSION

Slowly increase the intensity of the angling checks.

1
2
3
4

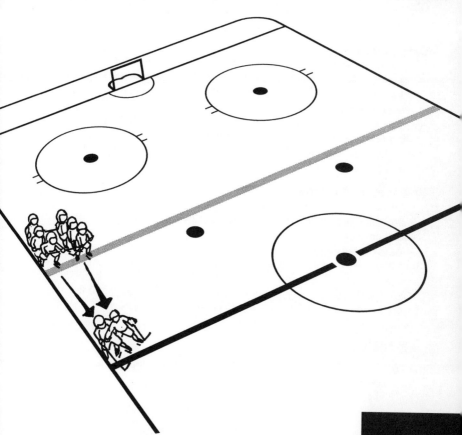

Direct Pinning Drill

Objective
To develop proper pinning technique.

Description
- Pair up players of equal ability and size in the neutral zone near the boards.
- Player #1 assumes a stationary position directly beside the boards without a puck.
- On a whistle, Player #2 attempts to pin him against the boards, but the first player does not try to get away.
- Player #2 keeps his palms up to control player movement both ways and to ensure that he is not called for holding.

Key Teaching Points
- Encourage controlled skating to close the gap.
- Promote good pressure on both sides of the opposing player's body.
- Ensure that there is no evidence of holding!
- Watch carefully for technique. The pinning player's stick should always be extended away from the pinning area to ensure that it does not get caught up with the opposing player.
- Ensure that the pinning player does not wrap his arms around the opposing player, as he will likely be called for holding.

EXPANSION

A second whistle starts a full-intensity contest where the pinned player tries to escape his checker.

1
2
3
4

DIRECT
PINNING DRILL

Bull in the Ring

Objective
To develop strong one-on-one physical skills

Description
- Pair up players relative to their size and ability and divide the pairs among the four corner circles with a coach at each circle.
- In each circle, Player #1 has a stick, Player #2 has no stick.
- Player #1 stands in the middle of the circle on the center dot.
- On a whistle, Player #2 tries to push the opposing player out of the circle while Player #1 tries to stay as close to the center dot as possible.
- Blow the whistle after five to ten seconds of play to ensure high intensity.
- Players switch positions at each whistle, trying both offensive and defensive positions.

Key Teaching Points
- Encourage a strong tripod stance by the puck carrier.
- Encourage the defensive player to keep two-handed pressure on the puck carrier.
- Encourage players to have knees bent for better power.
- Ensure players have good balance on both skates.

EXPANSION
- The offensive player controls a puck on the centre dot while being pushed out of the circle.
- The defensive player holds a stick during the drill as well. He should hold it with one hand while pushing but not crosscheck the opposing player.

1
2
3
4

BULL IN
THE RING

Corner One-on-One Drill

Objective
To practice narrowing the gap between defenseman and forward with good skating control

Description
- Divide players into two lines near the mid-slot area.
- The first player in the defensive line starts on his knees.
- On a whistle, the first player in the forward line retrieves a puck shot into the corner and tries to make an offensive play on the net.
- Delay the defenseman's forward movement at first, then have him narrow the gap to the offensive player in a controlled fashion.
- The one-on-one play continues until a goal is scored or the coach blows the whistle.
- Players switch lines after each play, in order to play both offensive and defensive positions.

Key Teaching Points
- Encourage proper timing.
- Encourage controlled forward skating by the defender.
- Promote agile movements.

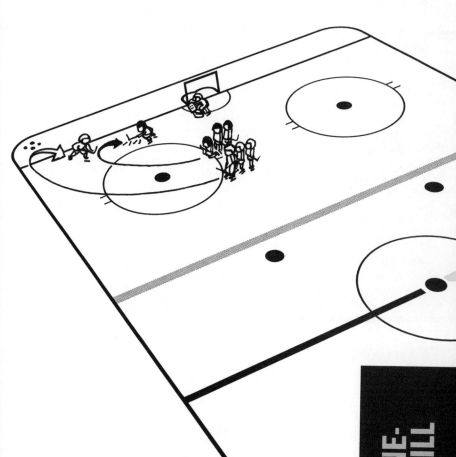

CORNER ONE-ON-ONE DRILL

One-on-One Front of Net Challenge

Objective
To develop physical presence defensively and offensively in front of the net

Description
- Divide players into two groups and place each group in a corner of the end zone.
- Designate one line of players as forwards and the other group as defensemen.
- A coach stands in the middle of the blue line with several pucks.
- On a signal, one player each from the forward and defense lines skate to the front of the net.
- Delay a point shot for a few seconds to allow both players to maneuver for good positioning in front of the net.
- Once the one-on-one challenge has progressed, shoot the puck on the ice for a tip-in.
- Play ends when the puck is frozen or goes into a corner. A new pair begins.

Key Teaching Points
- Encourage good balance with a tripod stance for forwards.
- Promote proper body position and stick control by defensemen.
- Promote good anticipation of the shot by the defensemen so that the forward's stick is controlled at the time of the shot.

EXPANSION

Defensemen play without sticks to encourage enhanced body position and strength.

ONE-ON-ONE FRONT
OF NET CHALLENGE

Defensive Drive Drill

Objective
To develop good defensive positioning going back to the net with forwards driving hard to the net

Description
- Line up the forwards in diagonal corners of the ice.
- Place the defensemen in two lines on either side of the center face-off circle.
- The first forward passes to the coach, who is standing stationary at the blue line, and then skates down the boards.
- One stride before the forward arrives at the center red line, the defenseman pivots and begins skating back to the far net.
- The forward receives a return pass from the coach and drives hard to the net.
- The defenseman skates directly to the near post and tries to intercept the forward.
- Set the timing so that the players reach the net close to each other.

Key Teaching Points
- Encourage full-speed skating.
- Control the timing—the focus is on the defensive player and proper checking technique.
- Ensure that the defenseman is just behind the forward for proper timing.

EXPANSION

The defensive player plays without a stick to increase the challenge.

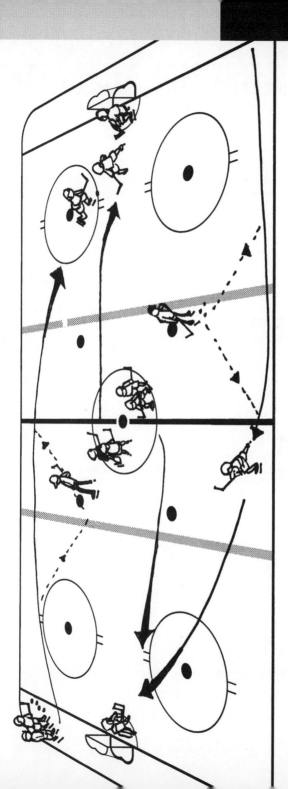

1
2
3
4

DEFENSIVE DRIVE DRILL

Around-the-Net Angle Drill

Objective
To develop proper timing and technique for the angling puck carrier

Description
- Divide players into two lines side by side at the blue line facing the near goal.
- The first player from the outside line shoots a puck at the goalie, who controls it and sets the puck up behind the net. The player, acting as a forward, skates behind the net and picks up the loose puck.
- The first player from the inside line skates slowly across the front of the net as a defensive player, gauging the offensive player's speed.
- The defensive player tries to angle the forward off towards the boards.

Key Teaching Points
- Encourage controlled defensive positioning.
- Start forwards skating at half speed, then progress to full speed.
- Ensure players skate at half speed early in the drill to practice technique, then increase skating intensity as they become more comfortable with the drill.

EXPANSION

Once the players have begun to master the skill of angling, set up a full-speed competition. The forward wins if he can reach the blue line with the puck.

1
2
3
4

**AROUND-THE-
NET ANGLE DRILL**

Full-Ice One-on-One Drill

Objective
To develop offensive speed versus defensive positioning

Description
- Divide players into two lines at each diagonal blue line, looking towards the near goal.
- Evenly place four to six pylons down the middle of the rink in the neutral zone to separate the sides of the ice.
- The first player from the outside line, acting as a forward, skates behind the net and picks up a loose puck.
- The first player from the inside line, acting as a defenseman, skates through the slot and pivots backwards.
- A one-on-one challenge takes place on both sides of the ice simultaneously.
- When both plays are complete, the next players from each end begin.

Key Teaching Points
- Encourage forwards to use speed changes and dekes.
- Encourage defense to try to stay between the puck carrier and the net.
- Encourage defense to always look at their opponent's chest, not at the puck.
- Encourage players to rotate from offense to defense each time.

EXPANSION

The defense plays without sticks, emphasizing the importance of proper body positioning.

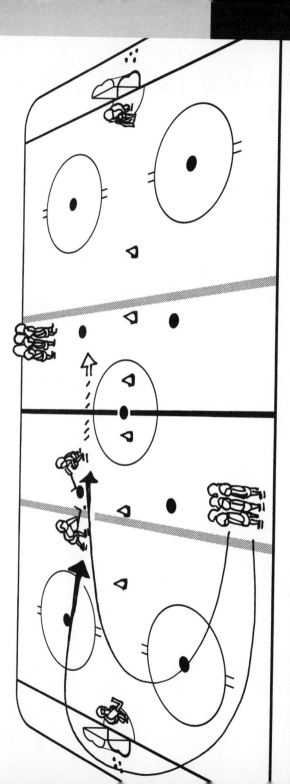

FULL-ICE ONE-ON-ONE DRILL

Two-on-Two Inside the Blue Line

Objective
To develop aggressive two-on-two skills

Description
- Divide players into two groups lined up outside the blue line and facing the net.
- On a whistle, two players from each group skate into the zone.
- Shoot a puck into the end zone to begin a two-on-two challenge.
- After 20 to 30 seconds, blow the whistle to stop the play.
- The next two players from each group immediately skate into the zone to begin, while the first two groups skate out of the zone quickly without touching the puck.

Key Teaching Points
- Encourage quick transitions between groups.
- Promote movement into open ice areas for passes.
- Emphasize high intensity and good one-on-one positioning.

TWO-ON-TWO INSIDE
THE BLUE LINE

One-on-One Defense Curl

Objective

To develop a defenseman's ability to close the gap and improve one-on-one checking technique

Description

- Divide the forwards into two groups located in the diagonal corners with the defensemen in two groups at corresponding blue lines.
- Place a pylon on the top of both circles, 5 meters (15 feet) away from the boards.
- A defenseman skates towards the forward line with a puck, makes a pass to the first forward and pivots around a pylon.
- The forward begins skating once he receives the puck.
  A one-on-one is begun and played down the side-ice area.
- The defenseman maintains proper one-on-one posture with knees and elbows bent and head up.
- Play continues until a goal is scored or the forward loses the puck.
- Rotate players between forward and defensive positions.

Key Teaching Points

- Encourage full-speed skating and good defensive positioning.
- Promote quick lateral movement and body fakes by the forwards.

Side-Ice Back-Check Drill

Objective
To develop good back-checking skills after an offensive rush

Description
- Divide players into two groups and have them line up in opposite corners of the rink.
- The first player from each line skates down the side of the rink with a puck.
- After taking a shot on the far goal, the player skates around the net and pursues the first player in the opposite line down the ice.
- The first player in the opposite line begins skating when the shooter is just skating behind the net.
- Continue until all players have had two or three turns, then repeat the drill from the opposite corners.

Key Teaching Points
- Encourage full-speed offensive attack.
- Promote quick recovery to back checking after a shot is taken on goal.
- Set up the timing so that the back checker is just behind the front skater.
- This drill is continuous and requires full-speed skating.

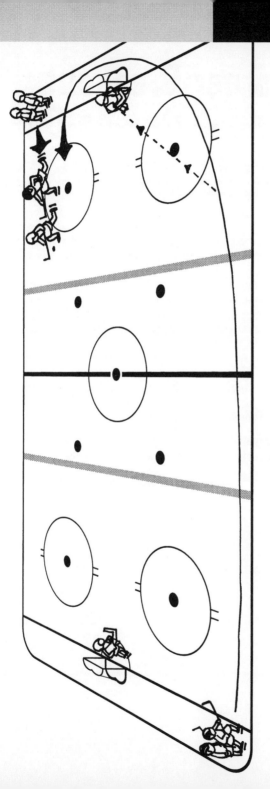

Four-Corner Breakout with Double One-on-One

Objective

To develop good defensive one-on-one skills with an emphasis on closing the gap between forward and defenseman

Description

- Divide forwards into two groups located in the diagonal corners of the rink, with the defensemen located in the opposite corners with pucks.
- On a whistle, a defenseman begins skating down the ice and passes a puck to the same-end forward who is also skating down the ice.
- The defenseman skates hard to as close to the centerline as possible and pivots backwards for a one-on-one against the opposing rushing forward.
- The forward continues skating down the side ice for a one-on-one attack.
- Play concludes with an offensive shot on goal or when the forward loses the puck.
- Another whistle starts the next play.

Key Teaching Points

- Encourage defensemen to make good passes and skate hard to close the gap.
- Encourage forwards to put full-speed pressure on the defense.

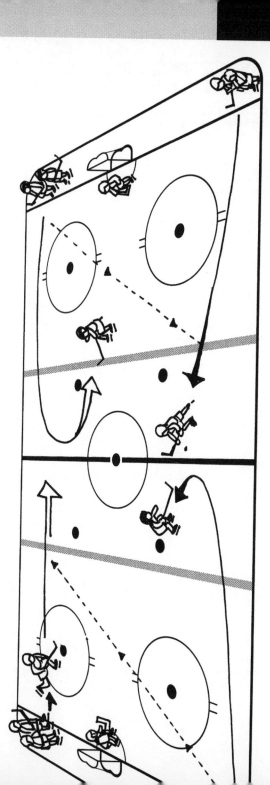

FOUR-CORNER BREAKOUT WITH DOUBLE ONE-ON-ONE

Two-on-One Circle Back Checking

Objective

To develop effective back checking in odd-man situations

Description

- Line up players in one corner of the end zone.
- Place one pylon just inside the centerline in the middle of the ice, another 2 meters (6 feet) closer to the net from the first, and a third pylon 2 meters (6 feet) out from the side boards just inside the near blue line.
- Player #1 acts as an offensive forward and skates around the far pylon.
- Player #2 acts as a back checker and skates around the near pylon.
- Player #3 acts as a passer, skates with a puck and curls to the outside around the close lateral pylon.
- Player #1, the offensive forward, skates hard to the net, attempting to get open for a pass.
- Player #2, the back checker, stays close to prevent a pass and any good scoring opportunity.
- Player #3, the passer, must pass at the proper time to the forward for a shot and a possible rebound.

Key Teaching Points

- Encourage the back checker to be aware of the puck as well as the player he is covering.
- Encourage agility and fakes by the offensive forward to get clear for a pass.

EXPANSION

The back checker plays without a stick to challenge him to attain even better defensive positioning.

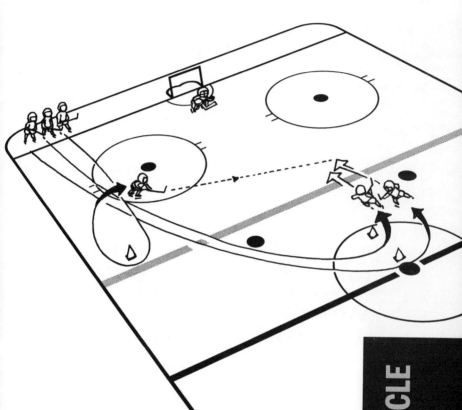

TWO-ON-ONE CIRCLE BACK CHECKING

Circle One-on-Two High Pressure

Objective
To help defensemen learn to close the gap when encountering a man-advantage situation

Description
- Divide players into lines on opposite blue lines facing into the defensive zone, with forwards in the outside line and defensemen in the inside line.
- The first player in the forward line skates behind the net and receives a pass from a coach in the corner of the rink.
- The first two defensive line players skate to the defensive circle hash marks and pivot backwards.
- When the defensemen reach the near blue line, one player reads the one-on-two play and skates towards the forward trying to put pressure on him.
- The defensemen try to angle the forward to the boards, using their two-on-one advantage.
- With speed, the forward tries to deke around the defenders for an offensive attack on the net.

Key Teaching Points
- Encourage communication between defensemen.
- Promote proper angling technique towards the boards.
- Players switch lines when they complete the drill in order to try both offensive and defensive one-on-two positions.

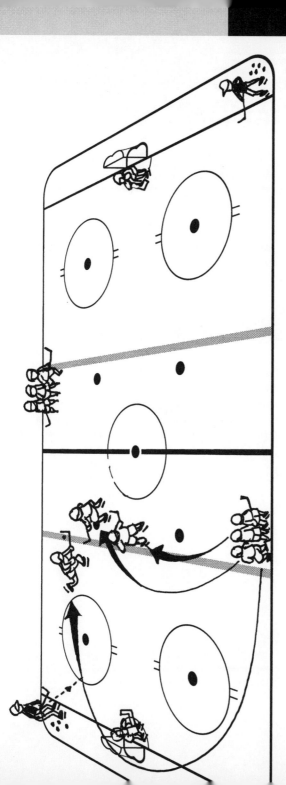

One-on-One Four-Shot Drill

Objective
To develop strong one-on-one physical skills

Description
- Form two lines of players outside the blue line and scatter four pucks inside the zone.
- On a whistle, the first player from the forward line enters the zone and picks up a puck, trying to score.
- The first player from the defensive line tries to stop the forward from attacking the net.
- When the forward takes a shot or loses the puck, he retreats to pick up another puck at the blue line.
- The defender reacts by closing the gap between himself and the offensive player.
- Continue play until all four pucks have been played.

Key Teaching Points
- Encourage the defensive player to stay in proper defensive position.
- Encourage the forward to continuously drive to the net with a puck.
- Blow the whistle if the tempo of the drill declines, and have two new players begin.

ONE-ON-ONE
FOUR-SHOT DRILL

One-on-One Circle Regroup Drill

Objective

To improve the ability of defensive players to close the gap on a one-on-one play

Description

- All defensemen stand inside the center circle in two lines facing the blue lines.
- Divide the forwards into two groups located on opposite diagonal blue lines.
- Place pucks in front of each forward group.
- Start each drill segment with a whistle to ensure that both sides begin at the same time.
- On the whistle, the defenseman at the front of each line skates towards the forward line and receives a pass. He quickly pivots backwards and returns the pass to the first forward.
- The defenseman quickly skates backwards to the far blue line, then pivots again to skate towards the centerline. On reaching the centerline, the defenseman pivots backwards again to prepare for the upcoming one-on-one play.
- Once the forward receives the return pass, he skates quickly around the entire center circle.
- Once around the circle, the forward and defenseman converge for a one-on-one play into the offensive zone.

Key Teaching Points

- Encourage offensive players to work on high-speed skating and lateral one-on-one moves.
- Encourage defensive players to close the gap to the skating offensive player, then make a quick transition to good one-on-one defensive positioning.

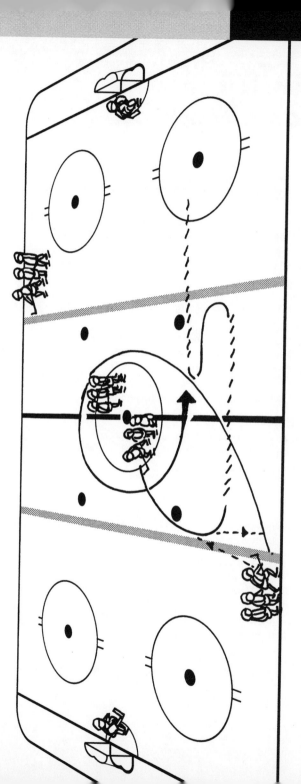

ONE-ON-ONE CIRCLE
REGROUP DRILL

Two-on-Two Defensive Transition

Objective
To improve defensive players' gap-closing technique

Description
- Line forwards up on each end of one blue line facing the near goal, while the defensemen line up on each end of the centerline.
- To begin, two defensemen line up directly on the blue line.
- One forward shoots a puck at the near goalie who attempts to control the puck, setting it up behind the net.
- The first forward from each line circles into the defensive zone, one skating behind the net to pick up the puck and the other skating just in front of the net.
- As soon as the puck is shot in, both defensemen quickly skate backwards to the centerline, then pivot and skate forward to effectively close the gap created between them and the advancing offensive pair. They then make a quick forward to backwards transition and the defensive pair is ready for a two-on-two challenge.

Key Teaching Points
- Encourage defensive players to make quick direction changes.
- Encourage offensive players to use inside-outside moves during one-on-one plays.

EXPANSION

The defensemen play without sticks in order to promote improved body positioning during the two-on-twos.

A second play begins once the first two-on-two play is complete. Both forwards and defensemen stay in front of the net, battling for a dominant position in front of the goalie. After 10 to 15 seconds of this positioning challenge, a coach or extra player shoots a puck on the ice towards the net. The forwards try to tip in the shot and the defensemen try to maintain good positional control.

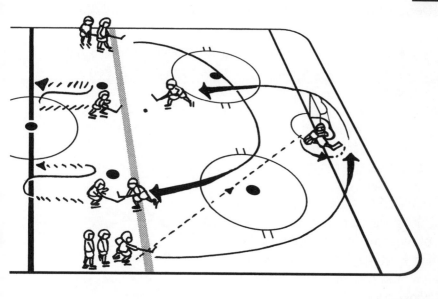

**TWO-ON-TWO
DEFENSIVE TRANSITION**

Defensive Zone Skills

Definition—*the ability to control puck movements in the defensive end of the rink*

GREAT COACHES OFTEN SAY THAT A GOOD OFFENSE STARTS with a great defense! Indeed, in order to begin an offensive play, a team must be able to control the puck in its own zone and easily break out using a team strategy. Many minor hockey teams rely on the natural talent of some of their players to carry the puck out of their zone. Unfortunately, as opposing teams become more skilled, this individual approach to defensive zone breakouts tends to fall apart.

It is wise for coaches at every level of play to consider beginning a teaching strategy that includes proper team-oriented breakout patterns as well as consistent defensive zone positioning. Coaches need not wait until players are thirteen or fourteen to begin teaching defensive zone strategies.

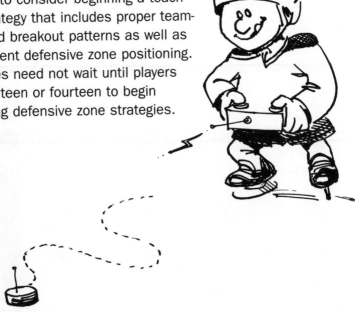

There are some simple, yet effective drills for eight- to ten-year-old players that will lay the foundation for defensive positioning drills they will encounter as they get older.

One of the keys to a successful breakout is to make sure that the players realize it is a breakout, not a breakaway. A winger or center who forces a pass by positioning himself too high in the zone or tries to break out of the zone too quickly not only creates confusion in the defensive zone, but he also runs the risk of getting solidly hit by an opposing defenseman before he ever reaches the neutral zone.

On the following pages are drills that focus on defensive zone skills.

DEFENSIVE
ZONE SKILLS

Defensive Zone Positioning

Objective
To develop proper positioning with offensive puck rotation in the defensive zone

Description
- Select a set of five players and line them up as if there is a center ice face-off.
- Point a stick to an imaginary puck being dumped in to one defensive corner.
- Players react to the puck movement by quickly skating to their proper defensive position.
- Rotate players back and forth from corner to corner by pointing the stick as if the puck is moving between the corners.
- Stop play to teach proper ice positioning for each position as necessary.
- Rotate players through each position so that all players can get a complete understanding of defensive hockey positioning.

Key Teaching Points
- Encourage quick transitions from one side of the defensive zone to the other.
- Promote complete awareness throughout the defensive zone.

EXPANSION

Add a quick forechecking rotation in the offensive zone following this drill.

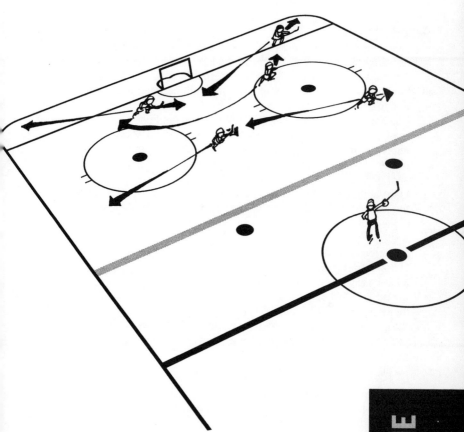

Shot-Blocking Drill

Objective
To develop proper technique of shot blocking for all age groups

Description
- Line up players at the top of a circle with the coach standing stationary at the blue line with a number of pucks.
- Tap a stick on the ice to signal that a shot is about to be taken.
- The first player in line tries to block the path between the coach and the goal.
- It is important to teach players to stack their shin pads directly in front of the puck and keep their hands high and out of danger. It is important to have good timing so that the player is on the ice no farther than 1 or 2 meters (6 feet) away from the shooter as the shot is taken.
- Players should always slide with their heads towards the center of the ice and feet towards the boards so that if a shot is faked, it is more difficult for the shooter to skate into the more dangerous middle slot area of the ice.
- Intentionally shoot the puck at half speed into the player's shin pads early on to give the players confidence in their sliding technique. Encourage players to focus closely on the angle of their shot blocking and the proper location of their shin pads with respect to the shooter's stick.
- As players' skill and confidence improves, increase shot speed.

Key Teaching Points
- Encourage players to become comfortable with blocking shots.
- Promote blocking in the shin pad area—timing is important.
- Encourage players to block a shot within 3 meters (9 feet) of the shooter if possible, to reduce the chance of an errant shot and possible serious injury.

SHOT-BLOCKING DRILL

Clearing Shot Out of the Zone

Objective
To practice effective clearing shots out of the defensive zone

Description
- Position players and pucks in one corner of the rink.
- The first player in line skates around the net and tries clearing a puck out of the zone.
- Players practice shooting hard off the boards or shooting high through the air.
- Use both sides of the rink, practicing both forehand and backhand clearing shots.

Key Teaching Points
- Encourage use of full power when shooting.
- Encourage use of the boards or shots high in the air as a tactical advantage.
- Emphasize full speed when players skate around the net.

Forehand off the boards

EXPANSION

Defensive players on the blue line try to stop the clearing shots.

High backhand

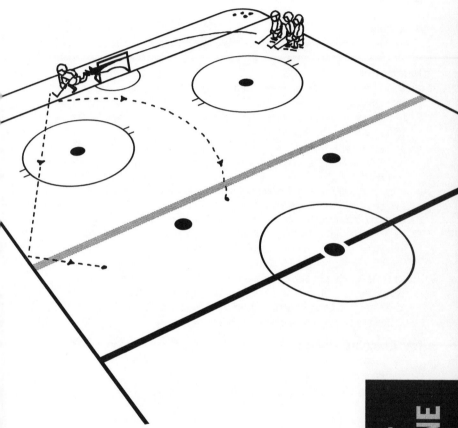

Five-on-Zero Breakout Drill

Objective
To develop effective team breakouts from the defensive zone

Description
- Select five players and have them line up as if there is a center ice face-off.
- Call out a breakout strategy (see pages 74–77) and dump the puck into one of the defensive corners.
- The wingers prepare to set up on the boards while the center follows the movement of the puck, making sure he does not get too far ahead of the puck.
- Players make quick, effective passes at full speed while progressing five-on-zero down the ice for a shot.
- Once the forwards have entered the neutral zone, a second coach passes an additional puck to one of the defensemen following the play.
- The defensemen pass the puck back and forth, stopping just inside the blue line until the forwards have completed their play on goal. Once a coach signals, one defenseman takes a low shot from the blue line.
- The three forwards stay directly in front of the net after their play, looking for a tip-in or rebound to finish the drill.

Key Teaching Points
- Call out the specific breakout (see pages 74–77) prior to dumping the puck in.
- Encourage full-speed skating and good positioning.

FIVE-ON-ZERO
BREAKOUT DRILL

Breakouts

1. Over Pass: Defense to Defense to Winger

The defenseman retrieves the puck from the corner and passes it behind the net to his partner. The second defenseman controls the pass and quickly passes the puck up to the winger who is standing on the boards facing the middle of the ice. The center follows the movement of the puck and receives a final pass from the winger to begin the offensive breakout. It is important that the pass to the center is short, only 2 to 4 meters (12 feet) in length, and is angled directly across the ice rather than up the ice. This will prevent the center from being hit by a pinching defenseman while looking backwards.

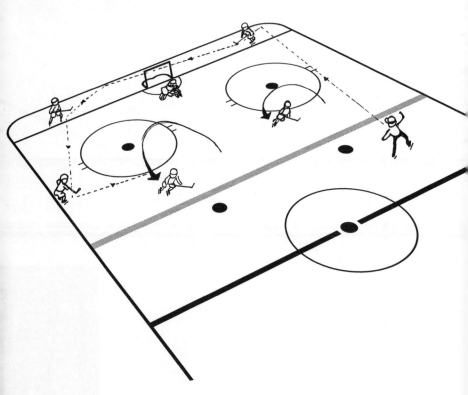

2. Boards Pass: Defense to Near Winger

The defenseman retrieves the puck from the corner and quickly turns towards the boards, passing the puck to the near winger who is standing on the boards facing the middle of the ice. The center follows the movement of the puck and receives a final pass from the winger to begin the offensive breakout.

3. Around Pass: Defense to Far Winger

The defenseman retrieves the puck from the corner and quickly passes it around the boards to the far winger who is standing on the boards facing the middle of the ice. The center follows the movement of the puck and receives a final pass from the winger to begin the offensive breakout.

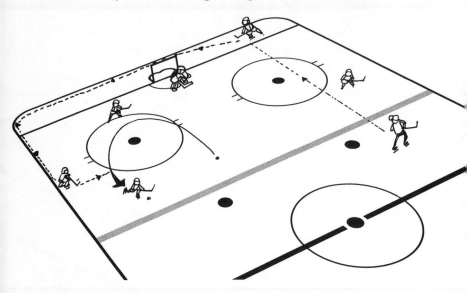

4. Quick Turn-Up: Defense to Center

The defenseman retrieves the puck from the corner and quickly turns up ice, passing the puck to the center who is circling deep in the defensive corner. The center then leads the forward line out of the zone for an offensive play.

5. Reverse Pass: Defense to Defense Reverse

The defenseman retrieves the puck from the corner and, while skating behind the net, passes it in a reverse direction to his defense partner, who skates into the first corner for the pass. The partner quickly passes the puck up to the near winger and on to the center for an offensive breakout.

Defensive Corner Breakout with One-on-One

Objective
To introduce team defensive zone breakouts

Description
- Line up players at the middle edge of the defensive circle in the end zone.
- Move the net down the goal line away from the player line-up.
- One player starts as a winger, beginning at the defensive face-off dot.
- Start the play by dumping a puck into a corner.
- The first player in the line acts as a defenseman and retrieves the puck, with the winger skating quickly to the boards.
- The defensive player makes a quick pass to the winger who carries the puck around both blue-line dots and re-enters the zone.
- The defensive player follows the winger, skating just up to the blue line, then aligns himself to play a one-on-one back towards the net.
- Once the one-on-one play starts, the next pair begins.

Key Teaching Points
- Encourage the defenseman to look for the winger's position before reaching the puck.
- Encourage the winger to have his back to the boards, facing out towards the whole ice surface.
- Encourage the defensive players to aggressively close the gap from the forward before the one-on-one play begins.

EXPANSION

Add a center who circles deep and receives a pass from the winger, then the center plays a one-on-one against the defenseman.

1
2
3
4

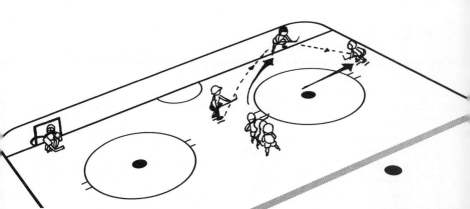

**DEFENSIVE CORNER
BREAKOUT WITH ONE-ON-ONE**

Triple Breakout

Objective
To encourage high-tempo defensive zone breakouts

Description
- Line up the offensive players outside the blue line facing into the defensive zone. Spread several pucks just out from the boards in both corners.
- A defenseman begins in the far corner of the defensive zone.
- The first forward acts as a winger and skates to the near defensive boards position.
- The defenseman skates behind the net with a puck and makes a hard pass directly to the forward.
- A second forward acts as a center and curls into the defensive end close to the winger for a short lateral pass.
- The center then skates the length of the ice and takes a shot on the far goal.
- A third forward acts as the opposite side winger and skates to the far defensive boards position.
- The same defenseman makes a hard pass in the opposite direction around the boards behind the net to this forward.
- The first winger skates across the slot and acts as a center, receiving a lateral pass from the third forward.
- The first winger then skates the length of the ice and takes a shot on the far goal.
- The same defenseman skates behind the net again, picks up a puck and passes to the remaining winger on the near boards. The winger then skates the length of the ice for a shot on goal.
- Finally, the defenseman picks up a free puck and skates down the ice for a fourth and last shot on goal.
- Begin the drill again with another set of three forwards and one defenseman.

Key Teaching Points
- Encourage the defensemen to make hard passes around the boards.
- Encourage the center to circle close to the winger for a short feed pass.
- Encourage wingers to control the pass with their skates if the puck has been passed around the boards.

EXPANSION
Shooters remain in front of net for tip-ins or rebounds from the remaining shots on goal.

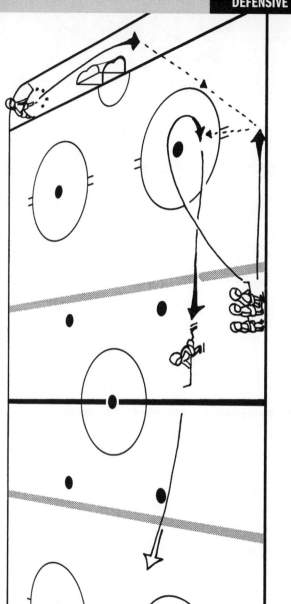

continued...

TRIPLE
BREAKOUT

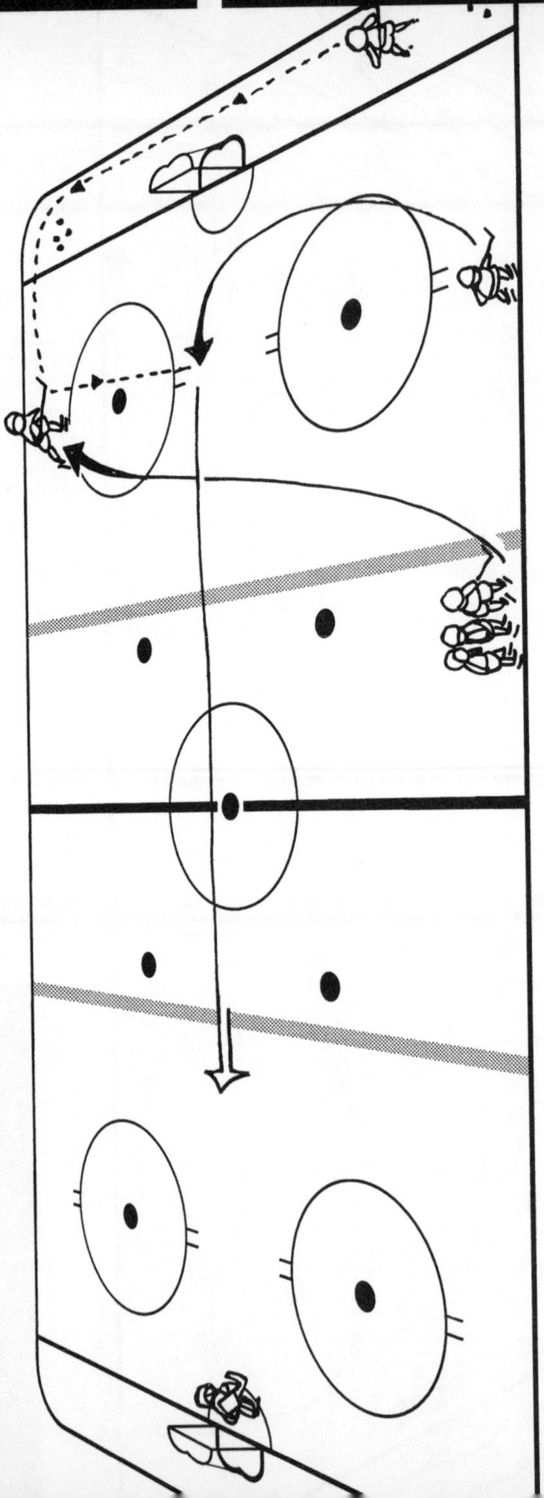

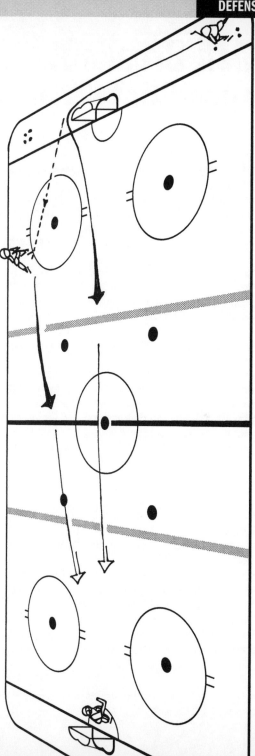

Three-Man Breakout and Return Shot

Objective
To improve defensive breakout technique

Description
- Divide players into equal groups of defensemen and forwards.
- The defensemen line up on one blue line facing the near goal, and the forwards line up at the middle of the blue line.
- The first defenseman starts the drill by taking a shot on goal from the blue line.
- The goalie controls the shot and sets up the puck behind the net.
- At the same time, the defenseman follows his shot to behind the net and either makes a direct pass or a pass along the boards to a winger standing near the boards.
- The first forward in line acts as the winger and skates quickly to the proper defensive zone position with his back to the boards at the hash marks of the defensive circle.
- The second forward acts as the center and skates more slowly into the defensive zone, circling near the winger as the pass is made from the defenseman in order to receive a give-and-go pass.
- Once the second pass is made, the defenseman and winger skate to the front of the net, ready for a tip or rebound.
- Upon receiving the puck, the center stickhandles around the mid-ice forward group and, as he returns across the blue line, takes a low shot on net.
- The drill is complete when all three players skate out of the end zone, and the next group can begin.

Key Teaching Points
- Encourage defensemen to pass the puck around the boards on the ice with good speed.
- Encourage forwards to control the boards pass with their skates while their backs are directly on the boards, their heads up and aware of any passes or opposing players in the area.
- Make sure the drill is performed from both corners of the defensive zone.

EXPANSION

Have a one-on-one challenge in front of the net between the defenseman and winger prior to the final shot being taken.

1
2
3
4

THREE-MAN BREAKOUT AND RETURN SHOT

Around the Net and Go

Objective
To improve breakout skills with quick return passes

Description
- Group players in three locations at each end of the rink—one corner in the defensive zone, one close to the hash marks on the opposite side of the ice, and one slightly farther down the boards between the blue line and the centerline.
- Position all pucks in the defensive corner with the first group.
- Player #1 takes a puck, skates behind the net and passes to Player #2 at the hash marks.
- Player #2 makes a quick return pass and then Player #1 passes to Player #3 outside the blue line.
- Player #3 returns the pass, and Player #1 skates quickly to the other end for a shot on the far goal.
- Once the play is completed, player rotation should be: shot on goal to outside the blue line to the hash marks to the defensive corner.

Key Teaching Points
- Encourage players to make passes while skating at full speed.
- Encourage attempts at soft one-touch passing.
- Encourage quick skating transition between lineup locations.
- This drill should be done simultaneously at both ends. Begin each drill with a whistle to ensure proper timing.

EXPANSION

Set up a pylon course for skating through the mid-ice zone after both passes are completed.

1
2
3
4

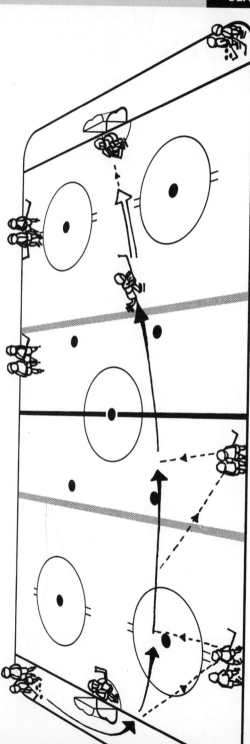

**AROUND THE
NET AND GO**

Offensive Zone Skills

Definition—*the ability to create scoring opportunities in the opposition's end of the rink*

GOOD DEFENSIVE STRATEGY ALLOWS A TEAM TO EASILY break out of their own zone. Once in the opposition's end of the rink, specific skills are useful to create goal-scoring opportunities. Skill in stickhandling, passing, shooting and coordinated team play ultimately determine if a team will be successful at scoring goals.

With the varying levels of skill seen in players at lower age levels, offensive prowess is often restricted to the one or two players who can regularly skate around their check and score a goal. Although entertaining, this type of individual effort does little to help players learn offensive team strategy. As these gifted players get older and the level of competition becomes more equitable, they often have trouble changing their offensive tactics, and they struggle to understand the concepts of team offense. Hockey is indeed a team game, and a player is never too young to learn the concept of intelligent team play.

It is often said that good goaltending backstops any opportunity for a championship. Unfortunately, not many teams will reach the ultimate goal of always playing to a 0–0 tie! Scoring goals with a creative and organized offensive strategy is the perfect complement to a solid goaltending effort.

On the following pages are drills that focus on offensive zone skills.

Offensive Zone Positioning

Objective
To introduce team offensive positioning

Description
- Line up players at center ice or after rotating in the defensive zone with Defensive Zone Positioning, pages 66–67.
- Point to one offensive corner to begin play.
- Players quickly forecheck an imaginary puck in that corner, establishing good positioning.
- Rotate the imaginary puck to the other corner while players make a quick transition.
- Repeat the rotation three or four times.

Key Teaching Points
- Encourage quick reactions to puck movement in the offensive zone.
- Encourage proper positioning of players when the puck rotates from side to side.
- Promote good awareness of players throughout the offensive zone.
- Encourage high-intensity skating as in a game.
- Stop the play as necessary to instruct on proper positioning.

OFFENSIVE ZONE
POSITIONING

Two-on-Zero Weave Drill

Objective

To improve passing skills while moving into openings on the ice

Description

- Form two lines of players in diagonal corners of the rink.
- The first player from each line skates down the boards with one puck between them.
- Player #1 passes to his partner, skates behind him, and moves to the other side.
- Player #2 passes the puck back to Player #1 and again skates behind him moving to the other side.
- The players make three or four passes down the length of the rink and finish with a shot on goal.
- Both players stop in front of the net for a possible rebound.
- The next pair begins skating when the first group reaches the center red line.

Key Teaching Points

- Encourage good, crisp passes onto the stick.
- Encourage quick lateral movement while skating.
- Promote proper lateral movement after making a pass.

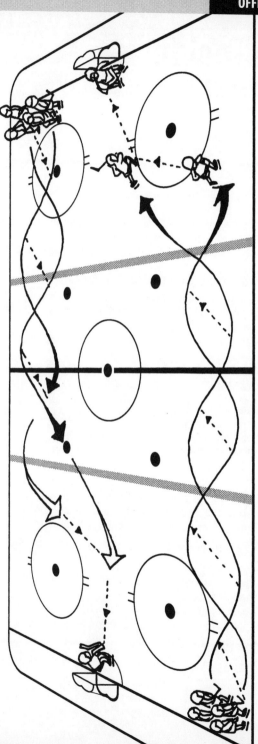

TWO-ON-ZERO
WEAVE DRILL

Side-Ice Inside Outside Drill

Objective
To improve lateral movement during offensive one-on-one plays

Description
- Divide players into two equal groups with pucks in diagonal corners of the rink.
- Three pylons in a slalom configuration are set up inside and just outside the near blue line on each side of the ice.
- Position a stationary coach at the far blue line on each side without a stick.
- The first player in each group stickhandles through the pylon course at full speed. When he approaches the stationary coach, the player tries to laterally fake inside. He then quickly gains speed and skates around the coach on the outside.
- Once past the coach, the player skates quickly to the net for a shot and possible rebound.
- The second player in each line begins the drill when the player ahead has reached the centerline.

Key Teaching Points
- Encourage players to skate at full speed.
- Encourage players to use full body lateral movement rather than simple head fakes.

EXPANSION

#1. Coaches hold an extended stick in front of themselves to get the players used to staying outside the reach of the defenseman's stick.

#2. Coaches actively pokecheck the players' pucks during each offensive rush.

#3. Players try to attack the triangle—move the puck between the coach's stick and skates rather than around his stick reach. Attacking the triangle formed by a defender's skates and stick blade is an effective strategy for forwards to catch defenders flat-footed, thus easily beating them on a one-on-one play.

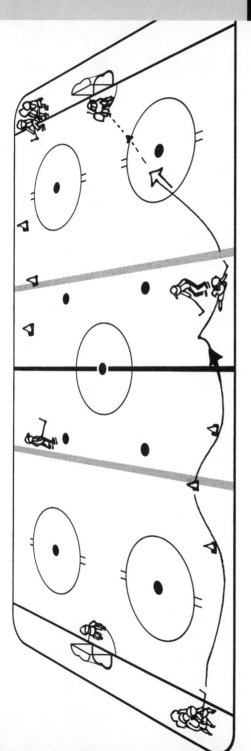

#1

#2

#3

SIDE-ICE INSIDE
OUTSIDE DRILL

Five-on-Zero Offensive Zone Passing

Objective
To practice good passing and rotations in the offensive zone

Description
- Set up five-man units in the offensive zone and establish proper fore-checking positions.
- Start the play by passing a puck to one player in the offensive zone.
- Players work the puck into both corners and out to the blue line.
- Encourage quick passes to teammates, with players reacting to changes in puck position.
- End the drill with a whistle after one minute with a shot on goal and rebounds.
- Extra players can practice face-offs, three-on-three in the middle zone, or long passing.

Key Teaching Points
- Encourage quick passes onto a receiver's stick.
- Encourage reactions to puck movement for proper ice position in the offensive zone.

EXPANSION

Add defensive players who play without sticks or with sticks upside-down to allow for easier offensive puck control.

Defense to Defense to Winger to Center Breakout and Shot

Objective
To encourage offensive breakout skill development

Description
- Line up the defensemen in one corner of the ice with the forwards at the near hash mark.
- Position one defenseman on the other side of the net and one forward at the far hash mark.
- Run the drill from both ends simultaneously and use a whistle to start each play.
- Begin play by dumping a puck into the close corner.
- The defenseman retrieves the puck and passes to the opposite defenseman behind the net.
- The far defenseman then passes to the winger on the boards, who passes to the first forward from the hash mark line-up who is breaking through the mid-ice zone.
- The first forward then skates hard to the other end of the rink for a shot on goal and possible rebound.
- Players rotate by following their passes to the next position and get ready for the next play to begin.

Key Teaching Points
- Encourage crisp, on-target passes between players.
- Encourage the center to always follow the movement of the puck in the defensive zone.

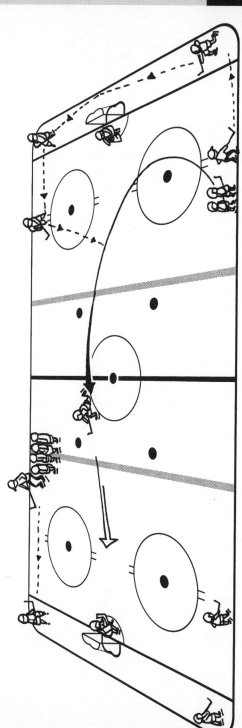

DEFENSE TO DEFENSE TO WINGER TO CENTER BREAKOUT AND SHOT

Offensive Drive Drill

Objective
To develop offensive players who excel at aggressively driving to the net

Description
- Position offensive players in two diagonal corners of the rink, with the defensemen lined up in the center circle.
- A coach at each blue line starts the play by tapping a stick on the ice.
- A forward skates full speed down the boards and passes a puck to the coach.
- The coach returns the pass when the forward reaches the centerline.
- A defenseman leaves his position when the forward is directly on the red line.
- The forward skates to the net with the puck while the defenseman tries to angle him off.
- The forward should try to use his inside leg to protect the puck from the defenseman's stick.

Key Teaching Points
- Encourage full-speed skating while protecting the puck.
- Encourage players to use their bodies to gain a positional advantage.
- Focus and timing is on the offensive player, unlike the Defensive Drive Drill, pages 40–41.
- Timing of the drill is important; defensemen should not leave too early.
- All players should practice both defensive and forward positions.

EXPANSION
The defensive player performs the drill without a stick.

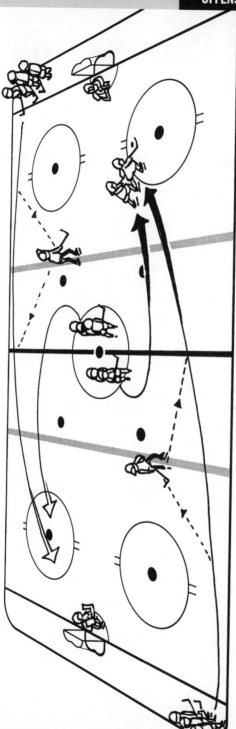

Forward Regroup Drill

Objective
To have offensive players practice coming back into the mid-ice zone for short, easy passes

Description
- Have three forwards line up at center ice, with two defensemen at the top of the defensive circles at one end of the rink.
- The center passes a puck to one defenseman, and the three forwards begin to skate back into the defensive zone.
- The defenseman with the puck makes a stationary pass to his partner while the forwards circle inside the blue line in the same direction as the puck movement.
- The defense partner makes a quick pass up to one of the forwards, and they then skate down the ice for a three-on-zero play on net, followed by a defense shot and a possible tip-in.
- The drill begins again with two defensemen at the far circles and a new set of three forwards at center ice.

Key Teaching Points
- Encourage forwards to always follow the defenseman-to-defenseman pass.
- Encourage short, crisp, easy passes from defenseman to forward.
- It is important that the forwards always turn towards the movement of the puck.

EXPANSION

Add one or two defensive players into the play in order to establish a three-on-one or a three-on-two challenge.

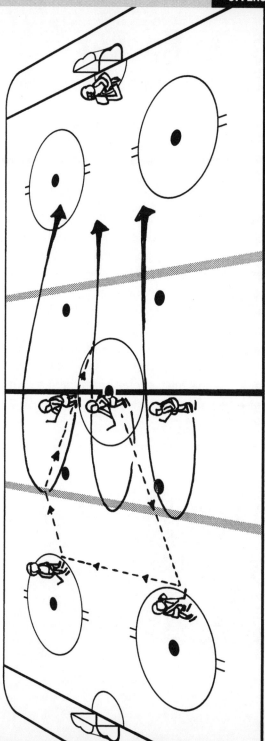

FORWARD REGROUP DRILL

Attitudes in Hockey

THE GAME OF HOCKEY HAS CHANGED GREATLY OVER THE past twenty years. Gone are the days of recreational skill development on an outdoor pond or rink with no coaches, fans or scoreboards involved. Hockey has become much more sophisticated, with multimillion dollar contracts up for grabs and with them, the inevitable pressures and ultimate disappointments.

Most people who reflect on the game and its importance in Canadian and North American society realize that the goal of amateur hockey should not be simply a route for sculpting players into NHL prototypes. The sheer number of participants in this great game demands the setting of loftier goals for our maturing players. Developing self-confidence and self-esteem, challenging one's discipline and determination, developing a healthy respect for opposition and officials, learning how to both win and lose like a champion, and most importantly, having fun—these are qualities that every hockey player must have the chance to experience and develop individually.

Why then, are so many hockey coaches preoccupied with solely teaching players how to win the game? Often overlooked is the fact that learning the intricacies of the game is an effective way to use a child's hockey experience to mold him into a responsible, caring, dedicated, disciplined, trusting and happy individual. Should this not be the ultimate goal in hockey? It is a goal attainable by all players, not just the best.

Some hardliners say that kids must be toughened up— skate them until they drop and punish them with endless skating practices for losing a game. Others wonder whether this attitude enhances a player's hockey experience or destroys it. If parents, coaches, managers and fans have clear goals for children in hockey, then with just a little self-reflection, the choice about what children should ultimately learn from the game is apparent.

This chapter is about focusing on the positive; it is about building attitudes in young men and women that will carry them throughout the rest of their lives. These are the less tangible skills that players come away with. This chapter provides suggestions that any coach can use to give every young athlete they encounter a positive hockey experience. Some of the ideas and concepts presented here may overlap. Many of these ideas and suggestions do bear repeating since they are so important for giving the children in your charge your best effort while asking them for their best.

ATTITUDES IN HOCKEY

Coaching Philosophy

Twenty years from now, few former Peewee hockey players will remember whether they came in first or second place in a spring hockey tournament. On the other hand, the memory of the sting at being verbally abused by a coach for making a bad play that cost the game endures, sometimes for the player's whole life.

Human memory is amazing, primarily because we remember significant events in our lives, and we tend to forget the seemingly unimportant ones. I can certainly attest to that. Only a few years after winning five Stanley Cup championships, I have a hard time remembering which team we beat to win each Stanley Cup. Don't even ask who we beat in the Campbell Conference Finals all those years! However, I will never forget the time when I was thirteen and my hockey coach, Wayne Gamble, asked me to go out and start his car after practice on a cold wintry day. What a thrill it was that one of my greatest role models showed enough confidence in me to toss me his car keys. Unfortunately, at 13, the only thing I knew about cars was how to turn the key. Little did I know that Wayne owned a vehicle with a standard transmission! Luckily my father was watching my attempts to start the car while it was in gear and came to my rescue.

Coaches have the power and the responsibility to instill character, confidence, respect and the ability to lead in every player during every season. In North America, if 20 hockey coaches were asked the secrets of their success, there would likely be 20 different answers. One of the beauties of life is the amazing variety of attitudes and approaches that can be taken to any task.

When it comes to coaching, however, there are ways that all coaches can provide the ultimate coaching experience for their players. These are:

- Plan fun activities for games and practices.
- Create a positive learning environment.
- Be consistent; treat all players fairly.
- Be well prepared for practices and games.
- Be a positive role model for your players.
- Work together with the opposing coach and the game officials to provide the most enjoyable experience for all the players.
- Include players in the decision making process during the season.
- Teach success as an attitude—players can learn as much from a loss as they can from a win.

Plan fun activities for games and practices
In order to keep young people playing hockey, coaches must ensure that they enjoy their experience. To do that, games that teach the skills of skating, balance, speed, conditioning and so on can be included in each practice. Teaching hockey skills as well as the intricacies of the game can be a great way to show children the camaraderie and spirit that develops in sporting teams. An environment of fun along with competition can only enhance their experience. Remember that the number one reason why kids play hockey is because they want to have fun with their friends!

Create a positive learning environment

Even the best NHL players make mistakes, both on and off the ice. So do young players just learning the game. Coaches must expect errors to be made during a game; however, responding in a positive way can turn mistakes into learning opportunities. Starting out with a positive remark before making constructive suggestions about ways that players can improve is a good way to take some of the sting out of what may be viewed as criticism.

A good rule of thumb is to try to give three positive remarks for every constructive suggestion or remark about an error! Players should never be afraid to make mistakes, because that is the only way they will learn and get better. Therefore, how the coach approaches a player will determine just what that player actually learns from a mistake. Will the player learn to play it safe in order to avoid making mistakes in the future or learn from the coach's suggestions and in a similar situation risk trying something new in order to improve his play? Coaches have a great deal of power over the way players handle their mistakes, both positively and negatively.

Be consistent; treat all players fairly

The best rewards a player can get from hockey are the feelings of excitement and companionship that come with being part of a team. As a result there is nothing more devastating to a team than when some players are treated differently.

It is natural that a coach might feel differently about certain players. There are players on every team who seem to know what the coach wants almost before it is mentioned and who learn concepts quickly and easily. There are also players who cannot seem to understand certain concepts or drills no matter how hard they try. Even though not all players are goal scorers or stars, each one is an important part of the team.

All players, even the favorites, sense when a coach treats their teammates differently, and that sends a wrong message to the entire group—that some players are more important to the team than others. While it can be difficult to treat all players the same way, even a player who does not have the skill to be on the power play may, with practice and patient instruction, become a valuable penalty killer for the team.

The best amateur hockey coaches believe that each player is as valuable as the next and should be treated as such! It is up to the coach to see that all players develop to their potential, and the only way that can happen is in a positive learning environment where all players are equally valued.

Be well prepared for practices and games

On a practice or a game day, coaches expect players to have their equipment on, their skates done up and be ready to hit the ice as soon as the Zamboni is clear. The players, meanwhile, should be able to expect that the coach is well prepared to run an effective, organized and efficient practice where they will have fun with their teammates and improve their skills. Planning for each practice, as well as long-term planning for the complete season practice schedule, ensures the best learning experience for all the players. A well-organized practice makes efficient use of time, keeps all the players moving and ensures that nobody gets bored during the session.

Many coaches have a general plan that they follow for each practice. They use specific drills to teach players the sequence of individual skills necessary to play the game, adding more difficult progressions as the players master the simpler drills and introducing more complex drills that closely simulate game situations. The Appendix contains sample practice plans and a blank template that can be photocopied and adapted to a coach's personal style.

Be a positive role model
Coaching hockey is a great opportunity to teach players the skills of the game. However, it is just as important to teach them about discipline, commitment, respect for the opposition and referees, fair play, and of course, how much fun the game can be. Coaches who are consistent and fair in their dealings with players, the opposition and the referees during the game quickly gain the respect of all the players.

By the same token, coaches who lose their tempers over bad calls, shout at referees or get angry after bad plays are also modeling those behaviors for players, who then assume that these behaviors are acceptable. As a result, it is no surprise when this coach's player takes a retaliation penalty or is ejected from a game for swearing. All coaches are role models for their players, and a coach's behavior influences players' behavior, after all. The choice between being a great role model or the opposite is obvious!

YA KNOW WHAT.. YOU'RE RIGHT! — IVE CHANGED MY MIND.

In response to a questionable penalty call, an inexperienced coach may yell at the referee, laying blame for disrupting the flow of their team's play. A more experienced coach who is in control of his emotions and aware of the effect his response will have on the players may say nothing. Instead, he will talk to the players about bearing down even harder to kill the penalty. With these actions, the first coach is indirectly showing players that questioning authority is acceptable and promoted on his team. The latter coach, however, is using a challenging situation during a game to teach players that they can conquer adversity with discipline, hard work and commitment, rather than by complaining.

Work together with the opposing coach and the officials

Even though the object of the game is to try to win, a strong coach can show team players that hockey is fun regardless of a win or a loss. A positive, upbeat attitude by all the adults involved means that both winners and losers can come away with a positive experience. Hockey experts do not judge a team's integrity and poise on how they win, but rather on how they handle losing, because invariably the best losers won't be for long!

Several simple strategies can show players that the opposing team and the referees are not their enemies, but rather an integral part of the game of hockey. Many teams will have their captains shake hands with the opposition coaches before the game. If coaches rotate their captains, then this gives all the players a chance to extend a gesture of fair play and respect to the opposition. Having all players shake hands with the referees at the end of the game is also worthwhile. By encouraging players to extend a hand to the officials after

the final buzzer, coaches are promoting the concept of fair play and also providing closure for that particular sporting endeavor. Any hard feelings can be forgotten, and players are more apt to remember the great plays and excitement of the game rather than any perceived bad penalty calls.

Meeting with the referees and the opposing coaches before the game often reinforces that all are in a similar situation, just trying to make the game as enjoyable as possible for the players. Personal contact allows both calm and aggressive coaches to keep involvement with their hockey team in perspective. Winning at all costs is good for no one, but rather, a high-intensity, close-scoring game that challenges players on both teams should be the ultimate goal. After all, neither the losing team nor the winning team benefits from an 11–1 hockey game!

Include players in decision making

Coaching is an important job. The coach is the overall leader who makes the decisions for the team—about who plays where and when, about the proper strategy for each game and about organizing good practices so that players get maximum benefit from their ice time. However, when it comes to minor decisions that do not affect the overall team plan, a strong coach tries to allow the players to become involved in the decision-making process. Cleaning up the dressing room, deciding what time players need to be at the rink before a game and whether to enter a tournament are decisions that can be made as a team. When players become involved in making decisions they become more accountable and more committed to the team.

Teach success as an attitude

Hockey is a game where 50% of the players in any given game will go home as losers on the scoreboard. It is an undeniable fact, yet it is possible to turn a loss on the scoreboard into a positive learning experience. After a game many coaches use the time in the dressing room as an opportunity to teach the players how to improve their play for the next game, rather than tell them how poorly they played. All teachers (including coaches) watch for the teachable moments; that is, the moments when a learner is most receptive or when the motivation to learn comes from within. The postgame talk can be this optimum time when coaches can boost sagging morale by pointing out all the successful plays during the game, in order to reinforce skill improvement. Drawing attention to ways that players or lines can improve their performance is important while the game is still fresh in their minds.

Rather than focusing on the disappointment of an overtime loss, experienced coaches can discuss the strong pressure the team had on the opposition before the goal was scored. They can point out how better execution may have resulted in a goal by their team and at the same time prepare players for a more consistent effort next game.

Following a 5–2 loss, experienced coaches will use their postgame talks to point out situations when the opposition scored and analyze how each player could react more effectively next time in a similar situation. They could talk about particular strategies on how to counteract the other team's strengths in the offensive zone in preparation for the next game. Finally, experienced coaches will comment positively on how well executed their goals were and single out players for their hard work throughout the game. Using this strategy, players will be disappointed with the loss but will leave the dressing room on an otherwise positive note! The cup can truly be half full rather than half empty; it all depends on the coach's attitude.

The Making of Great Players and People

If the only goal in the sport of hockey were to win every game, then coaching young athletes would be straight-forward. Coaches would try to acquire the strongest players, would hold practices every day and would try to schedule games against weaker teams in order to ensure success. This is certainly the goal of professional hockey organizations. However, most minor hockey coaches know that coaching a sport is also a valuable way to teach children important life skills.

Unfortunately, some players, parents and coaches see what occurs in the National Hockey League and believe that a similar attitude should filter down to minor hockey. Although the game is the same, other parallels between the National Hockey League and minor hockey should be avoided. The National Hockey League represents the pinnacle of hockey talent and excitement. There is only one goal during the games—to win. NHL players never enter a game saying, "Let's get out there and have a good game." On the contrary, because NHL teams are so evenly matched and are comprised of the best players in the world, each team believes that success naturally comes in only one way, with a victory. Many people also consider the National Hockey League to be a business rather than a sporting organization, with a dollars-and-cents bottom line rather than a focus on the guiding principles of the game. Experiments with pucks that glow like comets for the benefit of television coverage or the rumor of a change to four fifteen-minute periods to accommodate the media are just two examples of the compromises being made to Corporate America!

Compare the previously mentioned elite levels of hockey to minor hockey, where there is a wide range of skill levels and abilities, both between teams and within each team. Certainly one of the goals of any game is to try to win, and it is exciting to see young players trying their utmost to emerge as the victors in a weekend contest. However, for these young boys and girls it is just as important that, along with the game, they learn important life skills. If coaches remember why most children play hockey—to have fun with their friends—then winning naturally takes a lower profile.

After playing hockey for 30 years, I continue to confirm that in every hockey game across the country, barring ties, half the players win and the other half loses. Imagine the wasted time if those on the losing team got absolutely nothing out of the game!

Consider some of the life skills that all players can learn, whether they are on the winning or losing team. Some of these are:

- Self-Esteem
- Self-Confidence
- Discipline
- Learning How to Win and Lose
- Respect for the Opposition and Referees
- Having Fun

Self-Esteem

On examining society's problems with adolescents today, the list might include smoking, drug use, suicide, teenage pregnancy and poor scholastic performance. In each of these significant problems, a lack of self-esteem is implicated. The ability to think positively about oneself and one's future potential is a powerful force that can be used to keep young people moving forward in their lives. In hockey, where positive experiences and reinforcement from coaches can enhance a feeling of self-worth, it is possible to prevent these problems by taking steps to enhance self-esteem.

How can a coach help develop a heightened self-esteem in all players?

1. Focus on the positive aspects of a game—fun—not the negative aspects—losing.
2. Be less concerned about wins and more interested in improving skills.
3. Always try to make three positive remarks to a player for every negative comment or constructive suggestion.

Self-esteem cannot be bought; it is an inherent, inborn characteristic. It is affected negatively or positively by every experience we have in life, including hockey. Learning the game of hockey in a positive environment can be a valuable tool for enhancing self-esteem.

When I coach a hockey team, one strategy for improving self-esteem that I use is rotating the captaincy. Rather than assign the "C" and "As" to specific players, I select captains based on prior attitude, performance and effort. Knowing that in minor hockey, captains have virtually no role on the ice, I am not putting my team at a disadvantage by doing this. On the contrary, I give myself the opportunities to reward players for doing things that I believe are most valuable. I rarely award the captaincy to a player who scores three goals, because I want to show my players that team play is much more important than individual scoring pursuits. There are many instances when a weaker player can be singled out as deserving of the captaincy, even if that player is not a dominant goal scorer. A timely blocked shot, an energetic back-checking effort or an unselfish pass can often be the reason for making a certain player the captain for the next game. I keep track of which players have been captains and can easily make sure that each player gets equal opportunity to be a team leader. The ultimate reward for this strategy is watching a young person burst with pride at being singled out as a team leader. I know of no more effective way to boost a hockey player's self-esteem than with this simple tactic.

Self-Confidence

You may have observed a player just before a penalty shot who seems to be thinking, "I'm not very good at these," and then you watch the shot miss the net. It may be a cliché, but it is often said, "Those who believe they can and those who believe they can't are both right!" The ability to make young athletes believe that they are truly good hockey players, whether they are or not, is a skill that great coaches develop over the years.

Minor hockey is not just designed for the great players. It is imperative that all interested players have the opportunity to enjoy this exciting game and to develop self-confidence at any skill level. Some coaches complain that it is difficult to build up the confidence of a player who has poor hockey skills and seems to hurt the team on almost every shift. However, coaches who care about each member of the team remember that these young children are indeed just children. These coaches believe that the glory of winning is of lesser importance than the glory of seeing young people blossom in a sport that they are just learning!

How is it possible to build the self-confidence of a young, rather unskilled hockey player who hardly touches the puck during a game? Intuitive and observant coaches can always pick out certain decisions, plays or positions that a player has chosen that, although not producing a goal-scoring opportunity, can be identified as the proper play in that situation. A winger staying on the inside of the opposing defenseman in the defensive zone, a center anticipating a pass in the offensive end, or a defenseman following a scoring opportunity to the high slot looking for a rebound—all of these are decisions that can be rewarded with praise from one of the coaching staff.

Another effective way to improve the self-confidence of team players is to include a series of individual comments during the postgame talk. Making a positive comment about each player that focuses on some aspect of the game in which they performed well is important so that all leave feeling that they are contributing members of the team. If a coach does not have a positive comment about every player, then it is better to say nothing. What can a person say to a backup goalie who didn't even play in the game? "Great job! You didn't let one shot go by you!"

Discipline

Teachers would love the opportunity to teach a subject that students enjoy more than anything. All children become excited when they are able to choose what they want to learn. Coaches have a window of opportunity with hockey because those who are playing the game have chosen to be there. Thus, coaches have the chance to develop strong work habits, focused attention and self-discipline in their players. Like teachers, hockey coaches are valuable role models and must continually show athletes by example how important these habits and life skills truly are. Imagine the confusion brought on by coaches who demand punctuality before games and practices, but who are consistently late themselves. Or consider coaches who command the players to respect the referee's decisions, but who regularly shout and complain at what they think are bad calls. Discipline is a valuable skill that, once acquired, will be useful through-out life. Experiences in hockey can either enhance a player's disciplined attitude or destroy it!

It is a daunting task for coaches but they must realize that every single thing they do in the dressing room or on the bench will be scrutinized by 15 sets of eyes and ears. Every comment, every action, every bit of body language will be taken in by the players and processed and adapted to fit their view of life. Make sure that players see a consistent approach to the team goals and philosophies set out early in the season, not just from the head coach but from the entire coaching staff. If you ask your players to be enthusi-astic, be enthusiastic yourself; if you ask for discipline, be disciplined yourself; if you want them to have fun, have fun yourself!

Learning How to Win and Lose

From a coaching perspective, there's no question that it is easier to coach a winning team than a losing team. There are fewer complaints from the parents, the players are gener-ally happier and one's profile as an accomplished coach is enhanced. Many experts believe, however, that a player can learn more from a loss than a win. From the physical stand-point, playing against stronger teams pushes individuals to play to their highest potential, a situation that ultimately makes better players. As well, playing against teams that are highly overmatched provides little challenge and can potentially create a lazy, less committed attitude towards the game. If one reconsiders the fact that 50 percent of the time

a hockey player will likely be on a losing team, learning how to take something positive out of a loss is a valuable quality for all athletes. In a dynamic game like hockey, there are many good plays that intuitive coaches can emphasize, even from a poor performance. Unquestionably, coaches must point out mistakes in a calm, objective manner in order to properly teach young hockey players, but focusing on negative parts of the game simply because the team was outscored is not appropriate in minor hockey environments.

Respect for the Opposition and Referees

It has become quite fashionable in minor hockey circles to encourage players to hate their opponents. This kind of attitude is supposed to make them play harder and ultimately lead to more wins. Unfortunately, an attitude of hatred does nothing of the kind. In fact, it creates an environment where retaliation penalties are more prevalent and players lose their composure during the game, decreasing their effectiveness on the ice.

Hockey is not a game for the faint-of-heart—that's a fact. However, an environment of respect for the opposing team need not diminish the intensity of play. Some fans and coaches make the mistake of viewing an injured player on the other team as an opportunity for their team to win, rather than what it actually is—an injured child. A more objective observer in the same situation realizes that a young child has been hurt and that any hatred or aggression that caused the injury should not be tolerated.

As with opposing players, referees often bear the brunt of verbal assaults from players, coaches and parents. In almost all cases in minor hockey, these are young men and women who are just learning their skills (like the players and the coaches) and must be given some leeway when it comes to making mistakes. After all, if fans yelled and booed at every player who made a bad play in a game, they would likely be hoarse before the end of the first period! Young referees should be afforded the opportunity to gain their skills in a positive, supportive environment, free from criticism by adults who in most cases are only concerned about one thing—winning!

Having Fun

I am often asked what I consider to be the most important quality that will enable a hockey player to progress to elite levels—university, Olympic, or National Hockey League careers. Is it skating speed, discipline, determination, physical strength? It is true that all of these skills are important components in becoming an effective hockey player. But there is truly only one quality that will determine whether a child even has a chance to progress in this sport, and that is the ability to have fun.

For years I had the privilege of sharing the ice with some of the best players the game has ever seen—Messier, Gretzky, Fuhr, Coffey and others. I was regularly amazed that although these players were professional athletes and their job was to get back onto the ice each day for games or practices, they all brought with them an undeniable passion for the game they played. Often after practice most of the players could be found still out on the ice playing three-on-three mini-hockey, or a creative little passing game called "Pig in the Middle." I remember finishing our pregame morning skate at Madison Square Garden in New York. Six or eight of us were at center ice playing "Pig in the Middle," laughing and yelling at the challenge such a simple game provided for us. I looked up at the workers who were busy cleaning the stands in preparation for the upcoming evening event and couldn't help wondering what they were thinking while they watched us. Did they wonder how these professional athletes, pushed every night to perform at their best, could get such innocent pleasure out of the game they played? Since then I have come to the conclusion that likely the main reason why those players became such dominant superstars in the NHL was because they always had so much fun out on the ice!

Coaching Tips

Every player who has donned a pair of skates can think of a particular coach who has made a lasting impression in some way. It is hoped that this impression is a positive experience that makes a person's life richer and more fulfilled. Over the years I have had many coaches, ranging from minor hockey to professional levels. I can remember how each of these men had helped me become the best player I could be. However, one man stood above all others—a man who commanded respect from all his players by his sincerity, commitment, preparedness, consistency, and, above all, his integrity. It is no wonder that this man has become the coach with more wins than any other individual in collegiate hockey: Clare Drake.

Clare Drake exemplified the best in coaches—he wanted his players to achieve excellence, but winning games was a byproduct of his training, not the main goal. By watching great men like Coach Drake and others, I have tried to analyze the unique characteristics that make these people so special. All coaches should strive to provide positive experiences to all the young hockey players that they coach.

Consider this list of characteristics that all coaches should strive to be:

1. Be Positive
2. Be in Control
3. Be Prepared
4. Be Consistent
5. Be Fair
6. Be a Teacher
7. Be a Role Model

Be Positive

In the game of hockey there are many opportunities for players to doubt themselves. It is hard for players to be equally skilled in all areas of the game and sometimes their performances may suffer. If that player is in the National Hockey League, he may respond by going into a slump and beginning to second-guess himself. If that player is a minor hockey player, he may respond by quitting hockey and moving on to something else. Neither scenario is desirable, and a coach can help to prevent these occurrences by establishing a positive attitude in the dressing room and on the bench. There is a big difference between quietly correcting mistakes and yelling at a player who errs in the heat of intense play. Both strategies are commonly used in hockey rinks across the country.

Some say that the 1987 Edmonton Oilers team that I had the privilege to play on may have been the most talented hockey team ever assembled. I remember that even with all that talent we still lost 24 games that year. Coaches at the minor hockey level can never guarantee that their team will win every game, and therefore must gauge success not on winning but rather on skill improvement, team progress and enjoyment. A coach with a positive attitude can always find something good to say about a game or particular player, in order to conclude each event on an uplifting note. Even if the other team scores more goals, I often say, "Never tolerate failure, appreciate it!" Great coaches use losses to teach, motivate, refocus and prepare their players so that the effort put into playing the game is not wasted.

Be in Control

Have you ever seen a coach yelling and screaming at the referees or opposition and then turn to one of his players and berate him for losing

COACHING TIPS

his temper and taking a bad retaliation penalty? What kind of a mixed message does this give young players? Do they follow their coach's words or his actions? A great coach considers the effects of all his actions and statements long before he initiates them.

Staying in control after seeing a blatantly bad call shows the players that the coach has self-discipline and will not lose his focus for the remaining time left in the game. Coaches that motivate by yelling and verbally abusing players and others are quickly ignored. Any effect they have on their players is rapidly lost or shows up later in negative ways. In contrast, coaches who are objective, analytical and in control of their emotions gain the respect of their players permanently and, as a result, encourage a strong coach/player relationship. Emotional control is a skill that makes stronger teams but also helps to develop this important quality in players who are exposed to it.

Be Prepared
The coach expects players to be prepared to do their best during every practice and game. Skates in hand with a full set of equipment, the players have intuitively begun preparations for the event long before they hit the ice. In contrast,

many coaches come to practice with little forethought of what kind and sequence of drills to use during the ice time and why these particular drills should be run.

A simple practice plan, much like a teacher's lesson plan, is an easy but effective way for coaches to be prepared for and to lead a good practice or game. After all, a player is not much use to a team with only one skate; the same holds true for a coach who does not use the practice ice time effectively or runs an inconsistent bench during a game.

Sample practice plans and blank templates are available in the Appendix. These sample plans include warmups, drills and cooldowns that fulfill a specific practice objective. They may be photocopied and adapted for personal use.

Be Consistent

To play the game of hockey proficiently, a young player must master numerous physical and mental skills. This daunting task is made all the more difficult if players are coached inconsistently. Education in schools is based on a specific set of skills, and that curriculum is taught until the particular skills are mastered. This sounds familiar!

Learning in hockey is based on a specific set of skills, including passing, shooting, skating, checking and so on. These are taught repeatedly until the particular skills are mastered. It is crucial that the head coach and assistants understand all the hockey skills and teach them consistently. It is confusing for players to hear two coaches from the same team express completely different opinions on how to play the game. It can make a young player's head spin.

It is important that coaches meet at the beginning of the season to put together a comprehensive plan for team development, including routines for practices and games, skill development, fitness training and mental preparation. If this kind of long-term planning is done and if goals and routines are established early on, then the players will view the coaching staff as a unit and can begin the process of becoming a team, working together for success.

Be Fair

One of the most valuable life skills that we as coaches can teach our players is fairness. It is so important to believe that every young athlete on the team is inherently valuable and can contribute to overall success in a variety of ways. The National Hockey League uses role players on each team. These are fellows who may play only once or twice a period. Their job is not to be the goal scorer, rather just to fill an important space on a team that needs both superstars and grinders. Unfortunately, many inexperienced coaches see this strategy in the professional ranks and believe it should also be used in minor hockey.

There is only one reason why coaches preferentially play their best players and allow their less skilled players to sit out more frequently. That is to win, of course! There is nothing inherently wrong with trying to win games. In fact, part of the challenge of sports like hockey is to be able to rate oneself and one's team against the opposition. Unfortunately, many coaches overlook the price that is paid for trying to win at all costs. Imagine how devastating it must feel when a player's biggest role model in hockey, the coach, tells him to miss the next shift in order to put a better player out there instead. These seemingly inconsequential occurrences during a game are hardly remembered by the coach, but the effect on the player can be profound.

The solution is simple. Great coaches in minor hockey systems play all players equally. They teach their players to lose as a team. They teach them to win as a team. The notion of team building is a powerful concept, not only in sport but also as a legacy for school, family and business experiences in the future.

Be a Teacher

There are many roles that a coach must assume in minor hockey, including skate tightener, bus driver and friend. A coach must be able to run efficient practices and be able to control the flow of player changes during games. By far the most important role of a coach is to be a teacher.

Every young player deserves the opportunity to learn the proper hockey skills in a positive and enriching environment. In addition, invaluable personal qualities such as self-esteem, discipline, anger control, respect for opponents and being able to win and lose like champions can be taught to all hockey participants. When I am behind the bench or on the ice with my young players, I try to think of myself first as a teacher, second as a coach!

Be a Role Model

The highest compliment any hockey coach can receive is when a player comes back 10 years after playing on the team and says how fondly he remembers his hockey experience that year. In most cases players cannot even remember whether they won more games than they lost, but great hockey seasons are based on experiences much more important than simply winning or losing.

It is often said that a loss is only a loss if you don't learn anything from it! Great coaches can turn the worst season's record into a positive experience not soon forgotten by all players. To do so, coaches must become leaders, role models for every player on the team. If coaches show discipline, integrity and goodwill that we as parents hope our children will someday possess, then that goal becomes more easily attainable. Coaches are much like a mother duck followed by a brood of baby ducklings. If led to scream, blame, hate and be undisciplined, then the players will unhesitatingly follow. But if the coach leads by creating a spirit of camaraderie and fair play, respect for referees and opposition, winning and losing with honor and dignity, using hockey to have fun, then amazing things happen to the players involved!

Practice Organization

Many hockey experts believe a game is the worst place for a coach to teach new skills to players. The tempo of the game is fast and both players and coaching staff are usually preoccupied with the flow of the game, thus making learning new skills difficult. For this reason, good coaches use their practice time as effectively as possible in order to develop their players' skills in an atmosphere of learning and acceptance.

What sorts of things can a coach do to make practices most effective? Consider the following:

1. Have a plan.
2. Follow a consistent drill sequence.
3. Slowly integrate more advanced drills.

Have a Plan

Before every practice and game, all coaches ask their players to be ready with equipment and skates on, stick taped and minds focused on hockey. These same players have a fundamental right as well to have their coach prepared to run a well-organized, enjoyable, yet demanding practice. There is nothing more wasteful than seeing a coach show up ten minutes before practice with absolutely no idea what they will do on the ice. Often these practices turn into scrimmage sessions, which of course the players love but unfortunately do little to teach them any of the fundamental skills of the game.

Great coaches always write down an outline or plan for every practice that they run. Much like teachers who develop a lesson plan for each subject on each day, coaches can easily spend a few minutes prior to leaving for the rink to put some ideas down on paper. Not only does it organize one's thoughts about the team and where some of their weaknesses lie, it shows all the players that the coach is committed to helping the team become the best it can. Even if a coach is too rushed and cannot make a new practice plan, keeping a stock of old practice plans in a binder is a simple way of being organized. The Appendix contains sample practice plans to accomplish specific practice objectives and a blank template that can be photocopied and modified for personal use.

Follow a Consistent Drill Sequence

Mastering the skills of any dynamic game takes constant repetition during practice and improving execution during game situations. It therefore makes good sense to organize practices in a way that players of all ages can develop a rhythm of learning that simplifies the sometimes difficult task of acquiring new skills.

It is not uncommon for experienced coaches to establish a template for practices. They begin with a stretching and warmup drill, followed by a skating drill that may emphasize agility, speed or power. Following the natural progression of hockey skills, drills would then incorporate individual puck-handling, passing and shooting skills. Midway through the practice, the coach may schedule drills that work on team concepts: forechecking systems, breakouts, power plays and penalty killing. To end the practice, the coach may run the players through skating drills aimed at improving condition-ing. If a coach follows such a progression of drills, the play-ers soon begin to feel more comfortable with the flow of the practice sessions. Improved performance is likely. Making better hockey players by following a consistent practice drill sequence is assured.

Note: Coaches should consider saving their condition-ing skating drills until the end of practice for a number of reasons. The players tend to have more energy for the skill-related drills in the middle of the practice and a higher practice tempo is usually established. In addition, the ice surface is not damaged by hard skating early in practice, so stickhandling, passing and shooting drills can be performed on a much better quality of ice.

Slowly Integrate More Advanced Drills

Much like a teacher in a school, hockey coaches must pro-gressively stimulate their players to ensure that their skills continue to improve. Once a team has mastered a particular drill, experienced coaches add a slight technical variation or insert a more advanced drill in order to challenge the players at a higher level. Good practice drills are those that simulate game situations closely, and with the dynamic and exciting nature of the game of hockey, coaches can easily develop a series of drill progressions that can be used from novice to professional levels!

A Final Word

A great coach can teach players that the whole point of playing is not simply to win. Winning is such a limiting goal for an experience that can be so much more worthwhile. It is the coach's responsibility to ensure that all players leave their hockey encounter with something more than just the satisfaction of winning. The game provides the teacher/coach many important opportunities

- to develop technical skills,
- to improve the fitness levels of a group of interested individuals, and
- to teach important life skills such as self-esteem, self-confidence and discipline.

What an awesome responsibility! Responsible coaches realize that they have a tremendous influence over a group of impressionable bodies and minds, and that this influence endures long after the athletes leave their care. It is a coach's responsibility to ensure that not only do their players leave more skilled, but that they also leave as better people, with their self-esteem and confidence intact and a positive outlook that will carry them through life.

Appendix

Practice Plans

This appendix contains four different practice plans, each one aimed at developing a particular skill. These can be cut out or photocopied and used as a quick practice plan or can be adapted to your own personal style. Each practice plan is outlined for a 60-minute practice and includes suggested time frames for each drill. Each includes a warmup, a skating drill and then several drills to develop a particular skill. Practice sessions conclude with a time for closing remarks and a short cooldown skate.

It is important to finish every practice with a couple of positive words about the good things that were done on the ice. It is a great way to have the players leave the ice in a positive frame of mind. Conversely, if the effort at practice was poor, closing off the session with a word about the things that the players could do better at the next practice still leaves them with a positive reference and good direction for a more productive session in the future.

The cooldown laps are a good way of showing young players that, from a physiological standpoint, slowly cooling off with stretches and half-speed striding is a good way of allowing their muscles to recover after a hard workout.

Blank practice plans are reproducible and can be used to develop your own personal practice plans.

– Hockey Practice Plan 1 –
OBJECTIVE: Checking

Drill Name	From	To	Key Points
1. Double-Circle Warmup[1]	0	5	stretch/agility/ warmup
2. Fwd Backward Fwd Skating[1]	5	10	skating
3. Stick-Direction Drill[1]	10	15	agility/skating
4. Pairs Pylon Race[1]	15	25	skating/checking
5. Angle Boards Checking[3] –Telescoping Out & Back[4]	25	30	checking
6. Corner 1-on-1 Drill[3]	30	40	checking
7. Shot-Blocking Drill[3]	40	50	power
8. Showdown[4]	50	58	shooting
9. Closing/Two Cooldown Laps	58	60	feedback/cooldown

minutes

Notes:

---

[1] Book 1: *Skating Drills for Hockey*
[2] Book 2: *Puck Control Drills for Hockey*
[3] Book 3: *Team Drills for Hockey*
[4] Book 4: *Advanced Drills & Goalie Drills for Hockey*

– Hockey Practice Plan 2 –
OBJECTIVE: Team play

| | minutes | | |
Drill Name	From	To	Key Points
1. Double-Circle Warmup[1]	0	5	stretch/agility/ warmup
2. Full-Rink Skating[1]	5	10	line jump/one knee/squat one leg balance/ alligator roll
3. Parloff Relay[1]	10	15	agility/skating
4. Defensive Zone Positioning[3] –Down & Up Technique[4]	15	25	defensive zone awareness
5. Defensive Corner Breakout with 1-on-1[3]	25	35	easy breakout system
6. 5-on-0 Breakout Drill[3]	35	45	full team breakout options
7. Pig in the Middle[2] –T Drill[4]	45	50	passing/ quick reaction
8. 3-on-3 Half-Ice Mini-Hockey[4]	50	58	shooting
9. Closing/Two Cooldown Laps	58	60	feedback/cooldown

Notes:

[1] Book 1: *Skating Drills for Hockey*
[2] Book 2: *Puck Control Drills for Hockey*
[3] Book 3: *Team Drills for Hockey*
[4] Book 4: *Advanced Drills & Goalie Drills for Hockey*

– Hockey Practice Plan 3 –

OBJECTIVE: Advanced Passing

Drill Name	From	To	Key Points
	minutes		
1. Double-Circle Warmup[1]	0	5	stretch/agility/warmup
2. Eight-Dot Skating[1]	5	10	agility
3. Shadow Drill[1] –Butterfly Save Technique[4]	10	15	crossovers, skating
4. Blue Line Horseshoe Drill[2]	15	25	passing
5. 4-Corner Box Passing & Shot[2]	25	30	passing/shooting
6. Full-Ice Horseshoe Drill with Options[2]	30	40	stickhandling
7. Diagonal Pass & Shoot[2]	40	50	passing & receiving
8. Half-Ice Baseball[4]	50	58	agility/fun
9. Closing/Two Cooldown Laps	58	60	feedback/cooldown

Notes:

[1] Book 1: *Skating Drills for Hockey*
[2] Book 2: *Puck Control Drills for Hockey*
[3] Book 3: *Team Drills for Hockey*
[4] Book 4: *Advanced Drills & Goalie Drills for Hockey*

– Hockey Practice Plan 4 –
OBJECTIVE: Skating and Checking

Drill Name	From	To	Key Points
	minutes		
1. Double-Circle Warmup[1]	0	5	stretch/agility/warmup
2. Full-Lap Stick Relay[1]	5	10	speed/coordination
3. Stick-Jump Drill[1]	10	15	agility/fun
4. Bucket Relay[1]	15	22	skating speed
5. Defense-to-Wing-to-Center Pass & Shoot[2]	22	30	positioning/team play
6. 5-on-0 Breakout Drill[3]	30	40	team play
7. Around-the-Net Angle Drill[3]	40	45	checking technique
8. Direct Pinning Drill[3] –Mirror Drill[4]	45	50	checking technique
9. Full-Ice 1-on-1 Drill[3]	50	55	checking technique
10. Prisoner's Base[4]	55	58	agility/fun
11. Closing/Two Cooldown Laps	58	60	feedback/cooldown

Notes:

[1] Book 1: *Skating Drills for Hockey*
[2] Book 2: *Puck Control Drills for Hockey*
[3] Book 3: *Team Drills for Hockey*
[4] Book 4: *Advanced Drills & Goalie Drills for Hockey*

Hockey Practice Plan _____

OBJECTIVE: _____

Drill Name	From	To	Key Points
1.			
2.			
G—			
3.			
G—			
4.			
G—			
5.			
G—			
6.			
7.			
8.			
9.			

Hockey Practice Plan _____

OBJECTIVE: _____

Drill Name	From	To	Key Points
1.			
2.			
G—			
3.			
G—			
4.			
G—			
5.			
G—			
6.			
7.			
8.			
9.			

Drill Index

Acknowlegments

A special thanks goes to the members of the Titans from Sherwood Park, Alberta, their friends, friends of Randy Gregg and parent volunteer Elliot Chiles for helping with the photo shoot for the covers of these books.

Top Row (L to R): Matthew Willard, Randy Gregg, Jared Phillips, Trevor Brophy
Middle Row (L to R): Jared Semen, Jade Chiles, Michael Budjak
Bottom Row (L to R): Jeremy Rockley, Cassidy Monaghan, Donald Anderson, Brandon Chunick, Chase Elliott, Alec Chomik
Goalie: Travis Bambush

We couldn't have done it without you!